# RAC
# OVER FROM DOVER

## The BBC 'Breakaway' cross-Channel guide

## Roger Macdonald

D1390011

Published by RAC Motoring Services
in association with Dover Harbour Board

First published 1985 by RAC Motoring Services Ltd
RAC House Lansdowne Road Croydon CR9 2JA
Copyright © Royal Automobile Club 1985

Cartography by Kirkham Studios and the Royal Automobile Club
Typeset by Input Typesetting Ltd, Wimbledon SW19
Printed by Springbourne Press Ltd, Essex

ISBN 0 86211 050 5

Every effort has been made to ensure that the information given in this publication is accurate and up to date. However, the RAC cannot accept responsibility for errors or omissions, or for changes in regulations, prices or general conditions.

*Cover*
Mapping by George Philip Group
Photograph Colour Library International

# Contents

# Introduction

The milestones on the Dover Road that Charles Dickens counted off on his fingers on the way to the Continent; a species of fish called the Dover Sole renowned for its size and taste but rarely, one suspects, actually caught off the white chalk cliffs; a distinction shared perhaps only with London of having a French version of its name: Dover, or Douvres, has acquired a little niche of its own in British life.

Which is just as it should be. Dover has been the pre-eminent Channel port since Julius Caesar and the Romans based their northern fleet in its harbour some two thousand years ago; in medieval times it became a Cinque Port, privileged in commerce and protected by one of the most formidable castles in all England. If its military singificance disappeared with the 'Dover Patrol' of two world wars, Dover remains the focal point of cross-Channel trade and tourism. The port handles half the British tourists heading for the Continent by sea, as many as all the remaining passenger ports put together.

'Over From Dover' reflects the need for a travel book that is tailor-made for passengers leaving from Dover, that takes them step by step from their first, tentative preparations, into the heart of the French or Belgian countryside, or on to the vast network of European motorways.

What is different about 'Over From Dover' is that it makes no assumptions. Experienced traveller and novice alike can sometimes be thrown by the simplest problem or make the most obvious mistake – obvious, that is, only when you have actually made it. A good start does not guarantee a good holiday, but it goes a long way in the right direction.

## Acknowledgements

The ferry operators, Sealink and Townsend Thoresen, and the tourist offices of France and Belgium all gave generous assistance in the preparation of this book. However special thanks are due to Peter Mills of French Railways and Paul Youden of the Dover Harbour Board, whose help behind the scenes proved quite invaluable.

Roger Macdonald

# Before you leave

Minutes spent in preparation may save you hours of worry and delay. How to get the necessary documents and ensure your car is ready for the journey

## Passports and documents

By a curious quirk of history, the only people originally important enough to need passports, monarchs and representatives of monarchs, are now among the privileged few who in practice do not need them at all. The rest of us have to cope with the complicated procedure of obtaining a full passport, a British Visitor's passport, or a British Excursion Document, if we wish to cross the Channel to the Continent and be allowed to land on the other side.

**British Excursion Document**
Until August 1984, it was possible to spend up to 60 hours in France by obtaining a simple identity card from the ferry operator, who would stamp it prior to departure from Dover. But with unconscious irony, on the very same day that they reduced passport checks on most motorists crossing the border between France and West Germany, the French government began to insist on a much more official means of identity being produced on entry at the Channel ports.

In doing so, they damaged severely the concept of a spontaneous trip to France (though happily not to Belgium, see below) by which someone already on holiday on the South Coast would simply decide on the spur of the moment to spend a day or two abroad. The replacement for the identity card, the British Excursion Document, unfortunately cannot be validated quickly, unless you are in the habit of taking your holiday with your doctor or the local vicar. This is because, rather like the full passport itself, it has to be signed by a Responsible Person who has known you personally for at least two years, such as a policeman, doctor, Justice of the Peace, bank official, lawyer or minister of religion, and these may be few and far between at your seaside resort.

If you have the slightest inclination to visit France, therefore, arrange your British Excursion Document before you leave home. They are most easily obtainable from main post offices, but experience shows that ringing up in advance is a wise precaution, because not every counter clerk has one readily to hand, and asking for one on impulse can lead to frustration and delay. In the great List of Forms it is described as Misc.457, which can be useful to know if you live out in the country and the local post office has to order some on your behalf.

Like every passport issued since February 1, 1915, when crossing the Channel was presumably a rather more hazardous undertaking with the Kaiser's Grand Fleet lurking somewhere just below the horizon, the British Excursion Document requires a passport-size photograph of the bearer. It should measure not more than 2½in x 2in, and not less than 2in × 1¼in, and be endorsed by the Responsible Person as a true likeness. Do not paste it on the form, because the post office official has to see the endorsement first. He will also want to see documentary evidence of your identity, which can be a birth certificate (see box for how to obtain one), or a DHSS medical card, or a DHSS Retirement Pension Book or DHSS Pension Card No. BR464, when you take the completed form back to a main post office for its validation stamp. Incidentally, you must go in person; no one can collect it for you.

**British Visitor's passport**

The introduction of this rather tiresome procedure even for day trips to France makes it difficult to escape the conclusion that the shrewd holidaymaker bent on a trip to the Continent would be better advised to disregard the British Excursion Document and at the very least, take out a British Visitor's passport instead. To begin with, the Excursion Document is valid for only one calendar month from the date of issue, so if you decide subsequently to take another excursion, you would have to go through the whole process again, whereas the British Visitor's passport is valid for many more countries, including the whole of Western Europe, and for twelve months from the date of issue – which of course could well include much of the following summer. Secondly, the only differences in the documentation required are that you need two photographs instead of one, and you are asked to fill in an index card retained by the post office. Thirdly, if you should wish to cash cheques or traveller's cheques abroad a British Visitor's passport is much more readily acceptable for identification purposes. Last, but by no means least, it does not require a counter-signature on the original application form to confirm your identity, which saves a good deal of trouble.

However if you feel sure that you will only travel once to France in the course of a year, the Excursion Document is significantly cheaper, even allowing for impending price increases. Each Document costs £2, against £7.50 for the Visitor's passport. The charge for a Visitor's passport goes up to £11.25 if a married couple are included on the same form – which is not possible on the British Excursion Document; each person aged 16 or over on the date of travel must possess their own.

A husband and wife could therefore spend £48 a year in a form-filling orgy if they went to France once a month. That seems an unlikely scenario – travelling abroad to France once a year is much more likely. But many married holidaymakers fail completely to plan ahead and instead take out a British Visitor's passport, year in, year out. At current prices, by the end of a decade they will have spent £112.50 on successive passports, compared to a single charge of £22.50 for a joint, full passport valid for 10 years. The difference: £90, which would pay for a lot of duty-free goods.

**Full passport**

The reluctance shown by many people to obtain a full or standard British passport (cost for one adult: £15) is derived from their impression that it can take for ever to come, largely true in the peak summer months; and that it requires little short of a first-class university degree to fill in the forms correctly. This is simply not the case, although at first glance Form 'A', the basic application form, does look a little like a Kafka-esque game of ludo, with a series of black arrows that invariably bring you back to the paragraph you hoped was already disposed of.

Where the full passport application does differ from the British Visitor's passport form is in its absolute requirement for you to produce a birth certificate and, if you are applying for a full joint husband and wife passport for the first time, or a wife is applying for a full passport in her married name for the first time, a marriage certificate (to obtain a birth and/or marriage certificate, see box). The person countersigning your application to confirm your identity must also add his or her official stamp, which (curiously) is not required on the British Excursion Document.

However the greatest confusion undoubtedly lies in exactly where your application should be directed. The British Excursion Document can only be validated at a main post office (in person between Monday and Saturday) in England, Scotland, Wales and Northern Ireland; but, if you live in the Channel Islands or the Isle of Man, you must still go to the Passport Office. The British Visitor's passport can also only be validated at a main post office between Monday and Friday, NOT on

### Birth and Marriage Certificates

If you are uncertain of the location where you were born or married (well, it could have been a particularly good stag party the night before the wedding), and therefore cannot approach the local Registrar for a certificate, you can obtain a copy of one or both at £5 each from the General Register Office, St. Catherine's House, 10 Kingsway, London WC2B 6JP (Tel 01–242 0262 ext 2446/2447/2449). Applications by post take at least two weeks, but if you go in person between 8.30am and 4.30pm., you can collect a certificate in 48 hours. In Scotland, apply to the General Register Office, New Register House, Princes Street, Edinburgh EH1 3YT (Tel 031–556 3952). In Northern Ireland, apply to the Registrar-General, Oxford House, 49/55 Chichester Street, Belfast BT1 4HL (Tel 0232–220202).

Saturday mornings, in England, Scotland and Wales. But if you live in Northern Ireland, here, too, you must go in person to the Passport Office, and once again this applies to the Channel Islands and the Isle of Man.

In the case of a full passport application, if you send it by post, there are many apparent anomalies. For example, who would have thought that if you live in Hampshire the correct Passport Office for your application is at Newport, in Wales? And despite the allocation of Middlesex under London, most people who live in Kent are expected to apply to Peterborough? The complete list can be seen in the box (see p. 8), but further changes may follow local government reorganisation in major city areas.

Many applicants settle for a British Visitor's passport because they suspect, with good reason, that they have left insufficient time for a postal application for a full passport. Certainly between April and August, you should send your application at least four weeks before you intend to travel to have any hope of receiving your passport in time without a good deal of inconvenience. The only way to be sure of getting a passport quickly in the peak

## Where to apply for a full passport

| Apply to | if you live in |
|---|---|
| Belfast | Northern Ireland |
| Glasgow | Scotland |
| Liverpool | Cheshire, Cleveland, Clwyd, Cumbria, Derbyshire, Durham, Greater Manchester, Gwynedd, Humberside, Lancashire, Merseyside, Northumberland, North Yorkshire, South Yorkshire, Staffordshire, Tyne & Wear, West Yorkshire |
| London | Greater London, Middlesex, London boroughs in counties of Essex, Hertfordshire, Kent & Surrey |
| Newport | Avon, Berkshire, Cornwall, Devon, Dorset, Dyfed, East Sussex, Gloucestershire, Gwent, Hampshire, Hereford & Worcester, Isle of Wight, Mid-Glamorgan, Oxfordshire, Powys, Shropshire, Somerset, South Glamorgan, Surrey*, West Glamorgan, West Sussex, Wiltshire. |
| Peterborough | Bedfordshire, Buckinghamshire, Cambridgeshire, Essex*, Hertfordshire*, Kent*, Leicestershire, Lincolnshire, Norfolk, Northamptonshire, Nottinghamshire, Suffolk, Warwickshire, West Midlands. |

*except London boroughs

best time to go is not early morning, because long queues frequently form before the offices open at 9 am. Experience shows that the most propitious time to arrive is between 4 and 4.30 pm, when the offices close officially. Although the outside doors will be shut, once you have a number, you will be dealt with that afternoon; and human nature being what it is, your application may seem to be processed that little bit faster – because passport officers have homes to go to, as well.

However do not assume that the actual passport will be issued there and then; this happens only in cases of the most pressing need. In most circumstances – and the same applies to personal applications for birth certificates – the document will be ready to collect 48 hours afterwards.

If you applied by post and a passport has still not arrived with less than a week before travel, or you have some other query concerning an application, telephoning requires time and persistence. Expect the numbers of Passport Offices to be frequently engaged or to take a long time to answer. The best time to ring is the precise minute they open – 9am from Monday to Friday. Real emergencies, such as serious illness of a close relative abroad

### Passport Offices

| | |
|---|---|
| Belfast | 0232-232371 |
| Douglas, Isle of Man | 0624-26262 |
| Glasgow | 041-332 0271 |
| Liverpool | 051-237 3010 |
| London | 01-213 3344 |
| | 01-213 6161 |
| | 01-213 7272 |
| | 01-213 3434 |
| Newport | 0633-56292 |
| Peterborough | 0733-895555 |
| St Helier, Jersey | 0534-25377 |
| St Peter Port, Guernsey | 0481-26911 |

Application forms for full passports (and most amendments) are obtainable from main post offices, which with a few exceptions also issue British Visitor's passports and British Excursion Documents.

months is to go in person (or send the butler or some formidable maiden aunt) with all the necessary documents to one of the mainland Passport Offices, situated in London, Newport, Peterborough, Liverpool, Glasgow and Belfast. Most of them operate a strict queuing system and give you a processing number on arrival. The

requiring you to travel at short notice, will be dealt with at the London Passport Office up to 6pm on weekdays and between 10 and 12 Saturday mornings. At other times a recorded message tells you whom to ring.

## Children

Children need to have the correct documents, too; inadequate documentation could cause delays when you arrive at Dover, and at worst compel you to abandon the trip. If Baby Simon has not been added to mother's passport (ask for form C.A.P.), he will not be allowed to travel. Daughter Sarah cannot travel with her father even if she is listed in her mother's passport and actually has it in her possession; she either has to have a passport of her own, or to be added to her father's passport, for which her mother has to give written permission in advance. Children under 16 can be added to a brother's or sister's British Visitor's passport, but not if they are going to Belgium, Holland or Luxembourg. Children under 8 cannot obtain British Visitor's passports or British Excursion Documents if travelling without their legal guardian (who of course is *not* their schoolteacher), and a full passport would only be issued in exceptional circumstances. So-called children over 16 need separate passports, but a parent must sign their application form until their 18th birthday. If a child is to be included on the passport of a relative other than a parent, then the parent must write a letter of consent.

## Identity Cards

All of this makes the ease of visiting Belgium for up to 60 hours positively refreshing – you can still go on a whim, with the identity card from the ferry or jetfoil company, having had your photograph taken in the booth at the Dover Terminal (beware queues in summer). This has resulted in some loss of business to the French Channel ports, causing one local mayor to describe the restrictions placed by his government as 'using boxing gloves to swat a fly'. However, perhaps the

*The choice of travel documents*

French authorities had become concerned by the ease with which allegedly any travel document could be obtained in the UK. There was a man whose form was counter-signed by his milkman and authenticated by the stamp from the dairy . . .

| Points to watch |
|---|
| If your passport is due to expire between April and August, apply for a new one months, not weeks, in advance |
| Apply to the correct Passport Office – which may not be the nearest (see p.8) |
| If you need to go in person, beat the queues by arriving late in the day |
| If you need to telephone a Passport Office, ring at opening time |
| Make sure children travelling with you have the correct documentation |
| A British Visitor's passport does not require a counter-signature to confirm your identity: both a full passport and a British Excursion Document do |
| Except in an emergency, you can obtain only a British Excursion Document on a Saturday |
| France requires at least a British Excursion Document for entry; Belgium will still accept the old-style identity card instantly available |

## Car documents

If you are travelling by car, a passport on its own may not get you very far. You will need in addition:

Full valid driving licence (not provisional) and possibly an International Driving Permit
Vehicle Registration Document
International Motor Insurance Certificate.

without these documents you could be delayed or have your holiday spoilt altogether.

First, the driving licence. Unlike the UK, on the Continent there is no discretionary period to produce a licence if you are required to do so by the police and failure to do so could result in arrest because, strictly speaking, this is not an offence that comes into the category of those for which fines are levied on the spot. It is therefore wise to have your licence with you whenever you are driving. If you are hiring a car only the most disreputable companies would allow you to do so without a licence; and if they did so, you might well wonder whether this casual attitude also extended to the servicing of their vehicles. Many hire companies will refuse to rent a car to someone under 25 because young drivers are statistically the most likely to have accidents.

Younger drivers should also note that with the exception of Denmark, Luxembourg and West Germany, you must be 18 or over to drive in Western Europe. In Italy, if your car is capable of speeds of 180 kilometres per hour (112 mph), you must be 21 to drive it. In many Continental countries, riding a powerful motorcycle is also forbidden under 21 – the regulations vary from country to country, so check before you travel.

If you have lost your licence, or it needs to be renewed for some reason, apply for a new one (using form D1 from a post office) from a Vehicle Licensing Office. If you have any problems – for example your new licence has not arrived a week before you are due to depart – ring the general enquiries number at DVLC Swansea, 0792–72151. This number, as you might expect, is frequently busy; the best time to ring is when the office opens, at 8.15 am from Monday to Friday. The office closes at 4.30 pm from Monday to Thursday, and at 4 pm on Fridays; closed weekends.

### International Driving Permit

An International Driving Permit is essential if you are intending to drive in Spain, and in Italy it will relieve you of the need to carry an official translation of your UK licence (but if you *do* need that translation it can be supplied, free of charge, by the RAC). In Spain, it is theoretically possible to take the alternative course of action of having a Spanish translation of your UK licence stamped by a Spanish consulate, but as this is both time-consuming and more expensive, hardly anyone does.

The IDP requires one passport-size photograph, the production of your driving licence, and the completion of a simple form at any RAC office. It costs £2. If you cannot produce your driving licence, a check call to DVLC Swansea will be necessary before the IDP can be provided. The IDP is valid for one year from the date of issue.

### Vehicle registration document

Carrying your vehicle registration document is also essential. If you have lost it, you can apply for a new one by using form V62, which is obtainable from any Local Vehicle Licensing Office. The fee is £2 for a replacement document. If at a point close to your departure your registration document is somewhere in the post, you can obtain a temporary vehicle certificate from a Local Vehicle Licensing Office by producing the current tax disc and some proof of your identity, such as your passport. In the case of a new car, or one that you have recently purchased, you will probably be required to complete form V204. If the licensing office has access to your vehicle's complete details, for instance if you had applied to them for a tax disc in the normal way, they may ask you to complete a more detailed form, V379. Form V204 would not normally include such details as chassis and engine numbers, but it would be perfectly acceptable for use abroad in almost every set of circumstances.

If time is really short, the RAC can issue you with an International Certificate for Motor Vehicles (you will need to know your engine and chassis numbers) at any main office (open until 12.30 pm on Saturdays); the fee is £2. However this certificate carries no legal authority and might not be acceptable to certain Continental authorities should you be involved in an accident.

If you are hiring a car to take abroad, you will not normally be able to take the registration document with you, and a photocopy is not acceptable. What you need is an International Registration Certificate for a Vehicle on Hire (VE 103), obtainable, price 53p, from a motoring organisation. You should provide the full details, including chassis and engine numbers, of the actual vehicle you are taking to the Continent. The hire company is not required to endorse your application, unless you are travelling to Portugal, for which a special certificate is required, signed by the representative of the rental company and counter-stamped by a motoring organisation: they will supply this certificate free of charge. If you are borrowing a car and visiting Portugal, the same certificate would have to be signed by the owner. For other countries in Western Europe, a simple letter of authority is normally acceptable; but you would still need to take the vehicle registration document with you.

## Tax

If your tax disc is due to expire during your holiday, that will not concern any Continental authorities, but you may wish to avoid a technical offence back in the UK. You can apply to re-licence your vehicle in advance, the only impediment being a practical one, because for security reasons the tax discs are not sent out to Local Vehicle Licensing Offices much more than one month before the actual issuing date. You can apply as much as six weeks in advance of the date of use, but there is no guarantee that you will receive a disc more than three to four weeks ahead. When you apply, use the standard form V10, obtainable from post offices. Enclose a letter explaining the circumstances.

Local Vehicle Licensing Offices are open from 9 am to 4 pm on Mondays to Thursdays, and from 9 am to 3.30 pm on Fridays. In each instance, apply to your nearest office and not to DVLC Swansea. If you live in the Greater London area, the arrangement by which applications were handled in Dundee has been discontinued, and replaced by local offices in the London area. Swansea, does however operate a vehicle enquiry service – 0792–72134. The hours are identical to the licence enquiry service (see above).

## Insurance

There is a common misconception that because UK insurance is legally valid in the EEC, an International Motor Insurance Certificate, popularly known as the 'Green Card', is no longer necessary. Nothing could be further from the truth. All that your UK insurance will cover automatically abroad, no matter how comprehensive your UK policy may be, is the legal

| Points to watch |
|---|
| You must be 18 or over to drive in most of Western Europe |
| An International Driving Permit and a bail bond are essential for Spain |
| In Italy you will need an official translation of your licence |
| Carrying the car registration document is also essential |
| If lost – use form V62 |
| If in the post – use form V204 or V379 |
| If hiring a car – complete form V103 from the RAC |
| Apply to a Local Vehicle Licensing Office, not to DVLC Swansea |
| If making enquiries, still ring DVLC Swansea and at opening time |
| Remember to apply well in advance if your tax disc is due to expire during your holiday |

minimum – which, for British motorists, does not cover damage to property or to a driver's own vehicle. The Green Card is usually obtainable either direct from your insurance company or through your insurance broker, at a fixed rate depending on the length of your stay. However, if you have only third party insurance at home, or you are borrowing a car, it is possible to obtain fully comprehensive cover. Should your own insurers be unenthusiastic about extending your cover, Norwich Union issue a Green Card under an arrangement through Extrasure that gives comprehensive cover on any vehicle, irrespective of the cover in force on the owner's insurance.

### Bail bond

If you are visiting Spain, even comprehensive insurance is not enough in itself. You also require a bail bond, which is the technical term for a financial guarantee that the insurance company will pay up should you be held responsible for an accident. As the Spanish authorities invariably detain foreign motorists unless and until they are satisfied that any claims against them will be met, failure to take a bail bond could extend your holiday in a type of accommodation that you did not exactly have in mind.

# Preparing your car

Many motoring disasters on Continental holidays can be traced back in some way to inadequate preparation. The majority of people would be horrified at the suggestion that they should buy a house without any kind of survey, or a second-hand car without a good look at it; yet they sometimes approach their motoring holiday with a total lack of attention to detail.

The chances are that your car will be travelling long distances at sustained high speeds and carrying a heavy load. In the course of, say, a fortnight, it may be driven at least five times further than in a comparable period at home. The risk of a breakdown is therefore correspondingly increased, together with the cost and inconvenience of repair.

### That vital service

Prevention is better than cure. That garage service before you depart across the Channel is vital. If you are travelling in the peak summer period, you will not be the only person going on holiday; your friendly mechanic at your conscientious local garage may well be abroad too – probably by air on a package deal, because he knows exactly what could go wrong with any car about to be driven too far, too fast. So the garage may be short-staffed or have temporary help – as well as being extra busy – and mistakes are most frequently made under pressure.

In the nicest possible way, make a nuisance of yourself. Write to the service manager (don't 'phone), emphasizing how far you are travelling, before you take the car in for a service, and do book this service well in advance. When you deliver the car, go through a check list on what you want done with the service manager or the mechanic concerned and check that the list has been completed when you collect the car. The following items should be given special attention:

**Brakes**  Driving at high speeds or up and down mountains increases wear dramatically, so brake linings or pads should be carefully checked to ensure that the friction lining will last the trip. Unless changed in the last year or so, it is advisable to have the brake fluid replaced, especially if you are towing or going up and down mountains.

**Electrics**  The most common cause of breakdown is some kind of electrical failure. Make sure that the battery is charging properly and contains sufficient distilled water: check that the fan belt is not loose or showing signs of wear. Inspect all the electrical connections and use a demoisterising spray on the battery, distributor and plug leads. Run a check on all the lighting functions – side, head, tail, brake, indicator and reverse.

*A spare parts kit*

**Engine** The service should include a complete engine oil change and new filter. Spark plugs in use for 10,000 miles or more should be replaced. Particular attention should be paid to carburettor, fuel pump, petrol pipes, fan belt and water hoses. Anti-freeze strength should be checked if you plan any mountain driving, as temperatures drop sharply at high altitude.

**Tyres** Long journeys at high speeds put tyres under extreme stress, and it is essential that they should be maintained at the correct pressures – including the spare. Check the tyres thoroughly on both inside and outside walls for bulges or cuts; check tread area for foreign bodies. Ensure you have sufficient tread depth left to complete your journey with 2mm to spare. Remember that high loads, high speeds and high temperatures can increase wear rate dramatically. If in doubt, replace the tyre – it will cost much more in most places abroad.

**Spare parts**
Although you can, indeed should, take out an insurance policy that (if the worst comes to the worst) will ensure that you, your car and your passengers can complete your holiday or return home in the event of breakdown or accident – such as the Travellers Bond available from the RAC –

no insurance will miraculously repair your vehicle instantly at the roadside or produce a vital spare part out of thin air. To avoid delay, carry a set of common spare parts. If you intend to travel abroad regularly, and are not planning to buy a new car from another manufacturer, it may be cheaper in the long term to buy the parts outright. However, most car owners settle for an emergency kit, which can be hired quite cheaply if returned unopened. The RAC recommended touring kit, obtainable from Selectacar of Bromley (Tel. 01–460 8972), contains amongst other items a condenser, rotor arm, distributor cap, ignition coil, fan belt, set of plugs and points, set of spare bulbs, HT lead and even a tow rope – all parts which from experience are most in demand.

**Required by law**
If you dispense with a spare parts kit, you should stow some essential items in the boot (see box). Even if you are travelling only within Western Europe, some of the items are required by law. A first-aid kit is compulsory in Austria, Belgium, Greece and Yugoslavia, is almost universally carried in West Germany and is advisable in all European countries. In France, Spain and Yugoslavia you risk a fine if one of your lights goes out and you are not carrying a replacement. Italian police also expect you to carry a set of bulbs and regularly check foreign motorists. In Italy, too, it is compulsory for a visitor's vehicle to be

| Items to take | |
|---|---|
| Set of bulbs | Pair of windscreen |
| Set of fuses | wiper blades |
| Set of combination | Torch |
| spanners | Tyre pressure gauge |
| Wheel brace and jack | Foot pump |
| Fanbelt | First-aid kit |
| Insulating tape | Fire extinguisher |
| Tow rope | Warning triangle |
| Length of electrical | Spare can of oil |
| cable | Adjustable spanner |
| Spare can of water | Sparking plug |
| Pair of pliers | Contact breaker |
| Spare hoses | points |

fitted with an exterior rear-view mirror on the left-hand side of the vehicle. A fire extinguisher is obligatory in Greece, Belgium and warning a triangle is essential throughout Western Europe.

Other items that will be needed before you leave Dover include a headlight conversion kit, to change the direction of your headlight beam to suit driving on the right, and a GB plate. Because some drivers have been known to go abroad without one, or displaying a plate so small that it is almost illegible, Continental police now carry out occasional checks. By law the GB plate must be white with black letters, oval in shape, 4½in high and just under 7in wide. The letters should be just over 3in in height and ½in wide. Needless to say, the GB plate supplied by the RAC conforms to these dimensions.

## Hiring a car

Hiring a car to take or use abroad should be a straightforward operation, but needs thought and care.

Rental firms in the UK rarely suggest hiring a right-hand drive car for use abroad. They point out, correctly, that you are surrendering the principal advantage of renting on the Continent, that is, being able to drive a left-hand drive car, and that you are needlessly incurring the cost of transporting the vehicle from Dover across the Channel. Why not hire two cars, they

say temptingly, and have one waiting for you in Calais, Boulogne, Dunkerque, Ostende, or Zeebrugge. What they fail to point out is the hassle of taking all the luggage out of the first car on the UK side, struggling on to the ship or hovercraft, and repeating the process on the other side. You would then be faced with the prospect of going through the whole exercise again in reverse on the return journey. So think carefully before deciding on this option.

One problem involved in hiring in the UK is the fact that you do not have access to the vehicle registration document usually required abroad. For a solution to this, see page 11. Many companies also insist on your taking out vehicle recovery insurance, even if they are part of a multi-national organisation. Put simply, while they are happy to leave left-hand drive cars strewn the length and breadth of Europe, in the knowledge that once restored to good working order they can be rented out universally and will eventually be brought back to base, a broken-down or damaged right-hand drive car would daunt even a regular customer of that successful cut-price American firm, Rent-a-Wreck. Your rental company may give you another, left-hand drive car to use abroad if the right-hand vehicle is out of commission, but they will still expect you to return the right-hand drive vehicle to the UK.

If you decide to hire a car abroad, more or less any town of reasonable size will have offices of the major international rental companies. There are also local firms who will claim to be cheaper. Indeed, sometimes they are, but just as frequently they are not. A common strategy, especially in some Mediterranean countries, is to tempt the prospective customer with a low price that just happens to creep up when it is time to pay the final bill. International companies have extras too, but they can be seen clearly on the tariff.

### Insurance
A common trap is insurance. With many companies you will be offered insurance against personal injury and what is known as the 'collision damage waiver'. This is

the equivalent on your own policy at home of paying extra to have the insurers bear the whole cost of any repair. Personal injury may well be covered on your holiday insurance but a wise motorist will always take out the 'collision damage waiver'. With the smaller companies, make sure that these insurances are either included in the quoted price or find out how much you are expected to pay for them.

If you are in any doubt about the company's bonafides, ask to see their main insurance policy that confirms they are insured to run a rental business. Even in France and Italy, third-party liability can fall short of the cost of medical treatment and damages, should you be the innocent victims of an accident. In Austria and Switzerland there is still no national insurance bureau from which to seek redress if you are hit by an uninsured motorist. It is therefore vital to be driving a car that is itself fully covered against any eventuality.

Before you accept a car, check it thoroughly, starting with the bodywork, to make certain that any existing dents and scratches have been noted on the rental agreement. (Pointless, you might think, if you are taking out the 'collision damage waiver', but you are still obliged to report any accident to the rental company, so being able to distinguish between new and old dents is important.) Examine the tyres, estimate the tread, look for stones embedded in them, check the pressures of all tyres, including the spare – there might not even be one. Remove the jack and the wheel brace from the boot, find out where the jack fits, and try the wheel brace on each of the wheel nuts. Then sit in the car, examine the seat belts (if fitted) and see if your seat can be adjusted to a comfortable driving position. Switch on the ignition, test the sidelights, indicators and dip switch, windscreen wipers (the water reservoir is invariably empty), and the horn. With the help of one of the family, check whether brake lights are working. Then try the locks to see if your belongings will be safe in the car or the boot.

When you also ask for a test drive around the block to see what happens to the brakes during an emergency stop, the rental company will probably blow a fuse. Stick to your guns. Taking away a defective vehicle puts your life and those of your companions at risk, and if you do break down even the best international companies may take several hours to produce a replacement. Smaller firms may simply have no other cars to spare at all.

The next problem is the deposit. It is still possible to hire a car by leaving cash or your passport (though that is viewed with disfavour by many Continental police forces, and by the British consul), but most rental companies will expect you to produce a credit card and to sign the credit voucher before you drive away. In doing this you have virtually signed a blank cheque, making it all too easy for the company to increase the size of the bill, especially if you drop off the car when their office is closed. Although you may have some redress under the terms of the Consumer Credit Act if you use Access or Visa, settling a dispute can be a protracted and tedious business.

There is, however, a solution if you hire from one of the large international companies. Almost all of them have their own credit cards, which are easy to obtain, and which they prefer you to use because then they do not have to pay the percentage that goes to a credit card company. You sign a blank voucher in the normal way, but instead of the final bill being debited from a credit card account, it will arrive in the post like a standard bill, which you are expected to settle promptly. At this point – when no payment has been made – you will have an opportunity to dispute the total.

If you do decide to hire from a Channel port, select a company with an office close to the harbour. Efficient though rental firms are at meeting arrivals at airports, they seem strangely reluctant to offer a similar service in ports. Make sure that you have a written confirmation that they will meet you off the ship so that, if necessary, you can recover the cost of taxis, should they fail to turn up.

# The Dover Road

## The easy way to Dover from all around the country

The London Orbital Motorway, the M25, has already transformed the major strategic route to the Continent. Many drivers accustomed to using a port closer to home but with of course a much longer sea crossing, now realise that the opening of most of the M25 makes Dover a practical proposition even from East Anglia or the South West. What you may lose in miles, you gain in speed, for the Dover Road now offers an almost unbroken motorway run.

**From the North**
Both the M1 and the A1(M) have easy access to the M25 going east, that is, circling London in a clockwise direction. The section of the M25 linking directly with the M1 is not due to open until the summer of 1986, with a new M1 junction (6A) north

of the present junction 6. However even when it does, congestion seems likely at peak periods, and many motorists may prefer to keep to the present option for reaching the M25, which is to leave the M1 at Junction 7 and take the M10. This motorway leads directly on to the A405 and then the A6, both roads with dual carriageways, allowing drivers to join the M25 at its junction 23, South Mimms, (and eventually even earlier at junction 22). South Mimms is also the southernmost point of the A1(M), and where motorists using the A1 join the orbital motorway.

**From the East**
The M25 is joined by four major routes further east: the M11 from Cambridge, at M11 Junction 6, Junction 27 on the M25;

the A12 from Chelmsford at Junction 28; the A127 from Southend at Junction 29 and the A13 from London's dockland at Junction 30 – mainly roads of at least dual carriageway standard.

### From the North and East

All the converging motorists must now navigate the Dartford Tunnel which has toll booths in both directions just south of the Tunnel, and which, especially on Friday evenings and at peak holiday periods on Saturday mornings, may result in delays. Then, at Junction 2 on the M25, the direct route to Dover lies on the A2 going east on dual carriageway. Just before Rochester this leads straight on to the M2. Although the M2 reverts to the A2 and non-motorway status, the A2 by-passes Canterbury, scene of countless delays in the past, and provides dual carriageway for the rest of the route, apart from a brief stretch outside Dover.

### From the Midlands

Drivers lacking easy access to the M1 will be looking for an anti-clockwise route around the M25. The most promising point of entry for many will be via the M40 from Oxford (and eventually Birmingham), just before its southernmost point, at a new junction, 1A, which is junction 16 on the M25. From there the route follows the M25* (see map pp. 18–19).

### From the West

A new interchange on the M4 between Junctions 4 and 5 provides access to the M25 at its Junction 15. Further south, drivers using the M3 can leave at Junction 2 to join the M25 at what is its Junction 12. From here on, they can make use of a further long stretch of the M25 up to Junction 5.* From there motorists can take the M26, disregarding the Folkestone signposting, as it is a perfectly viable route to Dover. The M26 filters without effort into the M20, which provides the route for 11 miles skirting Maidstone, whereupon drivers should take the A249, 6 miles of

*by summer 1985

dual carriageway, to link on to the M2. The access, at what is Junction 5 on the M2, is by a tight upward spiral requiring considerable care. The route into Dover is now the same as from the North and East.

### Options

In the event of some advertised delay on the A2 or M2, the M20 presents a viable alternative. Drivers from the North or East can join it for its full length by continuing on the M25 clockwise around London until M25 Junction 3, and then follow signposts to Folkestone. There is a further option at Junction 3 on the M2, for at this point the M20 is only 3 miles away, reached on the A229, largely by dual carriageway. Drivers joining the M20 from the West by way of the M26 can of course remain on the M20 for the rest of the route if the M2 or A2 have delays. The one disadvantage of this route is the final stretch to Dover skirting Folkestone to the north, as the road is almost entirely single carriageway.

| Motorway driving |
| --- |

Even for experienced drivers, long journeys on motorways require special care. Lapses in concentration are common, especially when drivers are distracted by the presence in the car of members of their family. Frequent service area stops are advisable, even if the food rarely approaches a gastronomic delight**. Stopping on the hard shoulder of the motorway is strictly against the law, even if a driver is tired and wants to change with someone else or have a brief rest.

### Emergencies

If you do have to stop because of a breakdown or emergency, move the car as far away from the motorway as possible and switch on the hazard warning lights if you have this facility. Evacuate the vehicle as

** But note that there are no service areas yet on the M25 or M11.

*Overleaf: map of the M25 showing connections to other motorways and major roads*

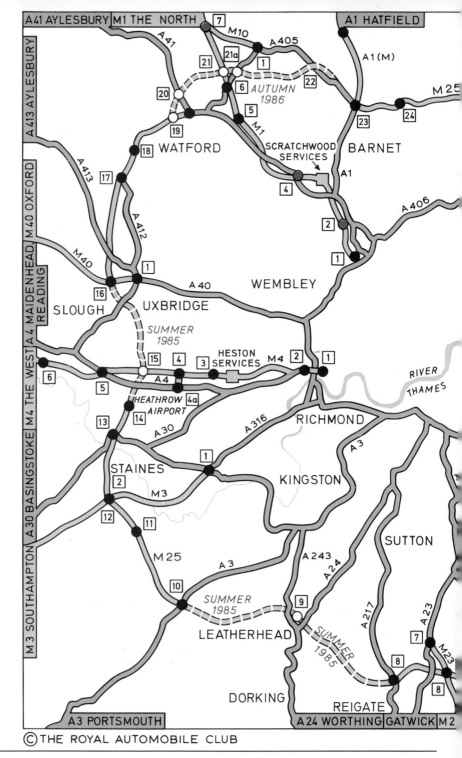

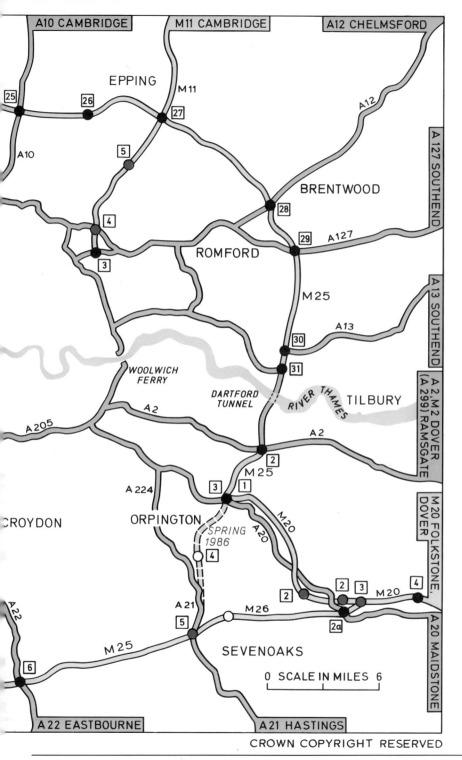

*The Dartford tunnel carries the M25 traffic under the Thames*

quickly as possible by the nearside doors, keeping a careful watch on children, and move the entire party up on to the bank. Place your warning triangle (which you had intended for Continental use) on the hard shoulder about 150 yards back from your car. If this seems like an excessive set of precautions, remember that many fatal motorway accidents occur when a vehicle is stationary on the hard shoulder.

When your car is empty, walk to the nearest emergency telephone; these telephones are connected to the motorway police control centre. You will be asked if you are a member of a motoring organisation; if so, the police will arrange for the organisation to help you. Otherwise they will contact a local garage, on a rota system, who will send out a mechanic complete with tow truck should the worst come to the worst. Towing is extremely expensive unless you belong to an organisation offering a free breakdown service, such as the RAC. Always return to your vehicle after using the emergency telephone. You can tell which is the closest by looking out for the small marker posts which are some 110 yards apart on the edge of the hard shoulder, and which carry an arrow pointing to the nearest telephone. Make sure that you take with you a note of your make of car, its registration number, and that you can give some idea of what has gone wrong. Police patrol cars will also radio for assistance if they see that you are in trouble and come to you on the rare occasions that the emergency telephones are not working.

# The Port

Through Dover to the Docks and on to your ferry

Motorists no longer pass through Dover as a kind of penance in anticipation of the Continental pleasures ahead. The days of long queues of drivers rushing desperately to catch a ferry, deaf to the complaints of the family jammed in the back, have undoubtedly gone for good.

Jubilee Way, a huge viaduct towering over the Ferry Terminal, connects the Port of Dover directly with the A2 and M2. It gives motorists a reassuring glimpse of their ship still securely anchored and awaiting their arrival and an escape road that perhaps serves as a timely reminder that it really is no longer necessary to take the last bend as though it were part of a grand prix.

At the bottom of Jubilee Way, a round-about leads into the Eastern Docks. To get your bearings, remember that with your back to the sea, the Eastern Docks are on the extreme right of Dover. Most ferry sailings go from here, but not crossings by hovercraft or jetfoil.

With your back to the sea, the Hoverport, the Western Docks and the Jetfoil Terminal are all situated on the left side of Dover. Ferry services to Dunkerque and some services to Ostende and Calais use the Western Docks, and this should be clearly marked on your ticket if you have made a reservation in advance.

From Jubilee Way, leave the roundabout at three o'clock to enter the Eastern Docks, or at nine o'clock for any other service. Although the route to the Western Docks complex would logically seem to be along the sea front into Marine Parade, all this will actually do is offer you a glimpse of the Dover Harbour Board's headquarters: access to the other terminals is by dual carriageway bearing right into Townwall Street, which leads eventually (by keeping left) into Snargate Street, from where the Western Docks, Hoverport and Jetfoil Terminal are clearly marked.

As this avoids most of the town's busier streets, it is the fastest route for motorists to reach the Western Docks if they have come to Dover by the M2 and A2. However, if you reach Dover by way of the M20 and A20, the A20 Folkestone Road offers easy access to the Western Docks.

# Eastern Docks

Although the Dover Harbour Board aims to make your journey through the Port as painless as possible, there is still one aspect of your journey that they cannot provide for you: the ferry tickets. If you arrive at Dover without an advance reservation, you should still go to the checkpoint where you

*The entrance to the Eastern Docks*

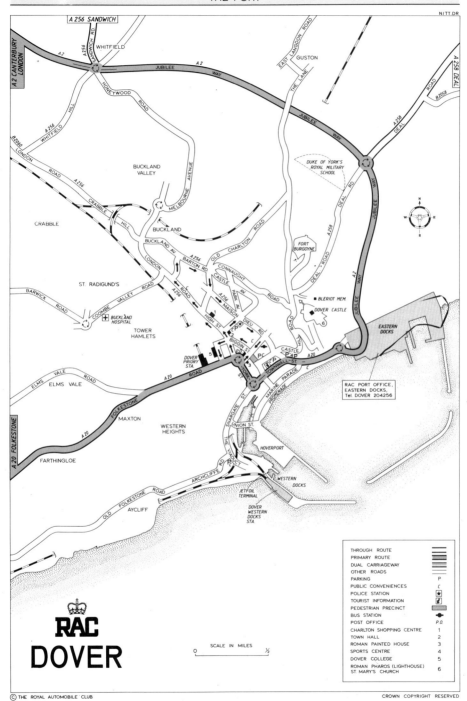

## RAC
## DOVER

SCALE IN MILES

0            ½

| | |
|---|---|
| THROUGH ROUTE | |
| PRIMARY ROUTE | |
| DUAL CARRIAGEWAY | |
| OTHER ROADS | |
| PARKING | P |
| PUBLIC CONVENIENCES | C |
| POLICE STATION | ★ |
| TOURIST INFORMATION | |
| PEDESTRIAN PRECINCT | |
| BUS STATION | |
| POST OFFICE | P.O. |
| CHARLTON SHOPPING CENTRE | 1 |
| TOWN HALL | 2 |
| ROMAN PAINTED HOUSE | 3 |
| SPORTS CENTRE | 4 |
| DOVER COLLEGE | 5 |
| ROMAN PHAROS (LIGHTHOUSE) ST. MARY'S CHURCH | 6 |

RAC PORT OFFICE,
EASTERN DOCKS,
Tel. DOVER 204256

will be advised on the first available ferry to your destination. All the sailings are displayed on a computer screen and the operator can make an instant reservation for you. He will then give you a form to take into the Booking Hall where you pay for your ticket. You do not have to return to the checkpoint.

If you have booked in advance, proceed in your car to the reception gates. The staff on duty will check your tickets and record your reservation and arrival on a computer. They will not, however, keep your tickets, because these are subject to a further examination by the staff of the individual ferry company. But that comes later. The Harbour Board official will advise you in the unlikely event of your ferry not running on schedule, and fix a small label to the windscreen of your car to indicate your destination. This ensures that no matter how hard you try, you will not find yourself in the wrong queue inside the Port.

You will also be given a letter, which reminds you of the route you should follow to the correct vehicle assembly area. However, all vehicles and passengers must first go through passport control. To reach this, keep to the left of the Booking Hall. In normal circumstances, the occupants of cars can remain in their seats and simply hand over their passports for a brief inspection by Her Majesty's Immigration (it's rarely called Emigration, even though you of course are leaving the country). Assuming all is in order, you will be on your way in a matter of moments.

From here on, follow your route letter. Routes are clearly marked, and if you do falter momentarily, officials are on hand to keep you going in the correct direction. They can see from the sticker on your windscreen which route and which company you are using, so there is no reason to worry. Do, however, remember that driving regulations are not mysteriously suspended inside the Port simply because, technically at least, you have already left the United Kingdom. There is a 20 mph speed limit, and several traffic lights.

Within minutes you will arrive at the vehicle assembly area. Cars are lined up in lanes and in strict order of priority, so the earlier you arrive, the earlier you are likely to board your ship, and it may also determine the order in which you disembark on the other side of the Channel. The outward sailing coupon in your tickets will be checked and collected while you are waiting by the staff of the ferry company, who will also give you a signal to drive on to the access ramps to the ship shortly before sailing time.

Motorists sometimes wonder why they are not allowed to board ships as soon as they arrive. One reason is that Her Majesty's Customs and Excise do not allow bars and duty-free shops to be opened on ship until 'Harbour Stations' have been called. As there is little point in having passengers milling around on board with no facilities to offer them, ferry companies delay embarkation until a short while before sailing time. Also, particularly in peak periods, ships are re-stocked and turned round so rapidly that there is barely enough time to get them ready for a fresh onslaught of passengers.

*Help and advice from the RAC at Dover*

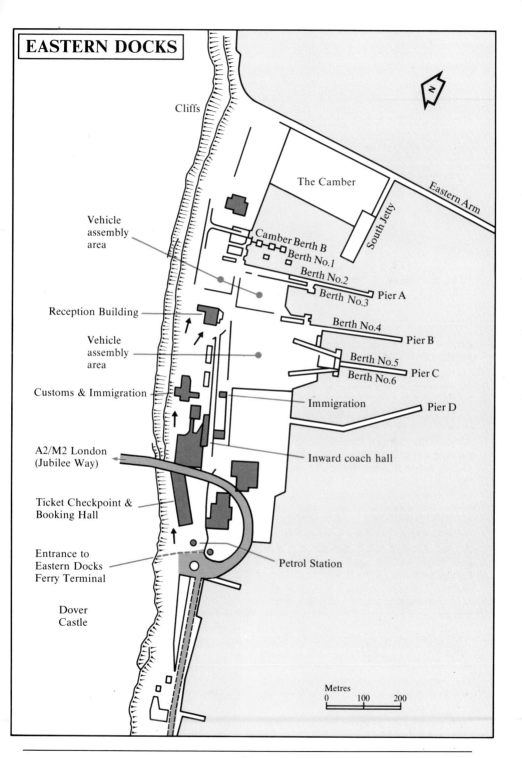

# EASTERN DOCKS

Cliffs

The Camber

Eastern Arm

South Jetty

Vehicle assembly area

Camber Berth B
Berth No.1
Berth No.2
Berth No.3      Pier A

Reception Building

Berth No.4
Pier B

Vehicle assembly area

Berth No.5      Pier C
Berth No.6

Customs & Immigration

Immigration      Pier D

A2/M2 London (Jubilee Way)

Inward coach hall

Ticket Checkpoint & Booking Hall

Entrance to Eastern Docks Ferry Terminal

Petrol Station

Dover Castle

Metres
0      100      200

*The Western Docks from the air*

## Western Docks

As with the Eastern Docks, motorists are checked in on arrival and directed to the vehicle assembly area, from where they go through passport control and on to the ferry shortly before departure. Tickets for passengers without advance reservations are obtainable from the Sealink UK Booking Office opposite Southern House. A cafeteria and toilet facilities are available in the Sealink car park or passengers can use facilities on the British Rail Marine Station. Trains from Victoria go through to Marine Station to connect with Dunkerque services.

## Jetfoil

The Jetfoil service operates from Admiralty Pier within the Western Docks. The check-in point for passengers is on Platform 4 at Marine Station. Passport formalities are completed immediately before embarkation. The Jetfoil does not yet offer a service to motorists.

## Hoverport

The International Hoverport operates in similar fashion to an airport. Although, as with the Eastern Docks, motorists are

*Jetfoil – fastest way to Ostende*

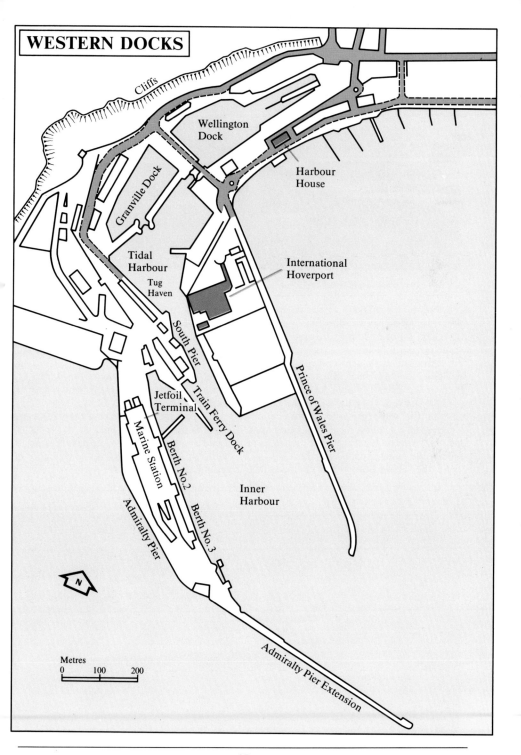

# WESTERN DOCKS

Cliffs

Wellington Dock

Harbour House

Granville Dock

Tidal Harbour

Tug Haven

International Hoverport

South Pier

Jetfoil Terminal

Train Ferry Dock

Prince of Wales Pier

Marine Station

Berth No.2

Berth No.3

Inner Harbour

Admiralty Pier

N

Admiralty Pier Extension

Metres
0    100    200

*Modern hovercraft can take up to 52 cars*

checked in on arrival, at the Hoverport they are given a boarding pass for each traveller before being directed to the vehicle assembly point. From there they go through passport control in their vehicles, as with the Eastern Docks, and then to the assembly area 'airside'.

Once parked, they have an opportunity to visit the duty-free and tax-free shop, which offers a much larger selection than the hovercraft itself, where space and indeed the journey time are short.

At the Hoverport other facilities are available in both the Concourse and the Departure lounges, including a cafeteria, a shop offering newspapers, sweets and related items, automatic change machines, telephones and toilets. There is a bureau de change which is open from 5.30am – 10pm in summer and from 7am – 6pm in winter.

For passengers not taking their vehicles, there is a limited car park at the front of the Hoverport. For foot passengers, as with an airport, baggage is checked in separately on departure.

*A hovercraft speeds into Dover*

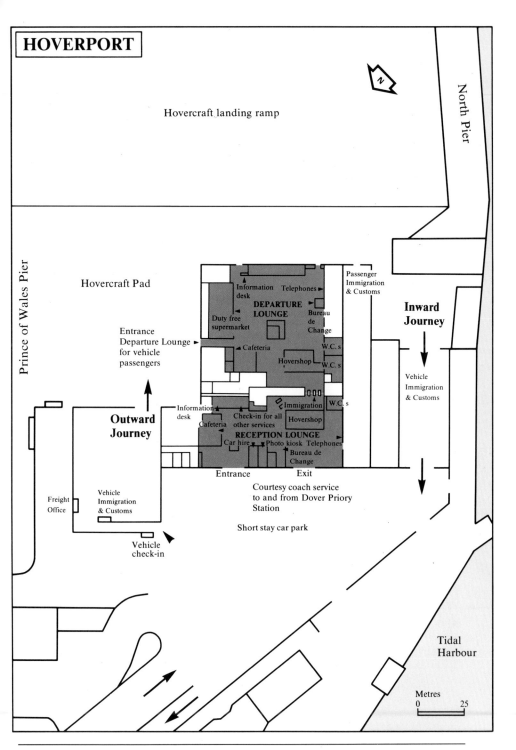

**HOVERPORT**

Hovercraft landing ramp

North Pier

Hovercraft Pad

Prince of Wales Pier

Information desk
Telephones
**DEPARTURE LOUNGE**
Duty free supermarket
Bureau de Change
Passenger Immigration & Customs

**Inward Journey**

Entrance Departure Lounge for vehicle passengers

Cafeteria
Hovershop
W.C.s
W.C.s

Vehicle Immigration & Customs

**Outward Journey**

Information desk
Cafeteria
Immigration
W.C.s
Check-in for all other services
Hovershop
**RECEPTION LOUNGE**
Car hire
Photo kiosk
Telephones
Bureau de Change

Entrance
Exit

Freight Office
Vehicle Immigration & Customs

Vehicle check-in

Courtesy coach service to and from Dover Priory Station

Short stay car park

Tidal Harbour

Metres
0          25

# Last-minute purchases

The Dover Harbour Board continues to extend its facilities within the Eastern Docks, and motorists will soon be able to rely on making purchases (other than newsagent's and tobacco products, which are already available) while waiting to board their ferry. However here is a list of shops where frequently forgotten items are readily available in Dover itself:

**Oil and Petrol**
Martin Walter, Eastern Docks (24 hours except Christmas Day, when there are no passenger sailings).
Western Docks Service Station, Snargate Street (not open Christmas Day): headlight deflector kits, GB Plates, tyre pressure gauges and other small motoring items also usually available.

The RAC Port Office located in the Booking Hall at the Eastern Docks can also supply warning triangles, first-aid kits, emergency windscreens, headlamp deflector kits, bulb kits, GB plates, maps, etc. It is open 24 hours.

Otherwise try Halfords (Biggin Street), Lucas (Russell Street) or the Unipart Centre (Castle Street).

**Banks**
Of the major clearing banks, Barclays, Lloyds and National Westminster all have branches in Market Square. Midland Bank has a branch in Biggin Street, a little further north. National Westminster also has a branch in the Ferry Terminal at the Eastern Docks which is open until 6pm in winter, until 10pm at busy periods, and 24 hours during the peak period of the summer school holidays.

Bureaux de change are available near No. 4 ferry berth at Eastern Docks, at the Hoverport and at the Western Docks. All the ferries have bureau de change facilities on board.

**Chemists**
Include A. A. Beggs in Pencester Road and Boots in Biggin Street.

**Post Office**
In Biggin Street, where you can obtain a British Excursion Document or (except on Saturdays), a British Visitor's passport. However, for the snags, see pages 5–6.

**Passport Photos**
Photographic booths are situated in the Concourse Lounge of the Hoverport; in the Marine Station, Western Docks; and in the Booking Hall of the Eastern Docks.

**Parking**
Street parking is difficult in the centre of Dover, where a one-way traffic system operates and double yellow lines abound. The closest car park to the principal shops lies just north of market square but is frequently full. A multi-storey car park (open 24 hours) is located off Russell Street, close to the Townsend Thoresen office, ½ mile from Eastern Docks.

For motorists leaving their cars in Dover, Relyon Car Parking of Poulton Close are open 24 hours and provide a mini-bus service to and from the Eastern Docks.

**Car Hire**

| Company | Location | Freephone |
|---|---|---|
| Avis | outside Booking Hall, Eastern Docks | Arrivals Hall, Eastern Docks |
| Godfrey Davis Europcar | Passenger Concourse, Hoverport | Arrivals Hall, Eastern Docks Platform 5, Marine Station, Western Docks |
| Hertz | Snargate Street | Arrivals Hall, Eastern Docks |
| Kenning | Maison Dieu Road | Arrivals Hall, Eastern Docks |
| Swan National | Townwall Street | Arrivals Hall, Eastern Docks |

# Cross-Channel pioneers

## From early days to the invention of the hovercraft

*Boarding the ferry the hard way*

The French Revolution provided the biggest stimulus to cross-Channel traffic, with many a French aristocrat, fleeing to escape Madame Guillotine, finding a fresh hazard at Calais or Boulogne, where he might be hoisted aboard an English fishing boat, complete with coach and horses, under cloak of darkness. Despite the fanciful creations of Baroness Orczy, it seems probable that the success of the ensuing voyage depended more on a liberal offering of golden guineas than on the ingenuity of the Scarlet Pimpernel.

Such crossings were, however, clandestine and depended entirely on a favourable wind. It was not until after the defeat of Napoleon that a steamship crossed the Channel. On 17 March, 1816 the 38–ton *Élise,* having picked up passengers at Greenwich and Dover, left Newhaven for Le Havre. It was not an auspicious beginning, as the ship ran into a storm. The journey took 17 hours, the passengers and most of the crew were sea-sick, including the captain, Pierre Andriel. Captain Andriel, it is believed, was not an experienced cross-Channel skipper. He was simply delivering the *Élise* to her new Parisian owners, as she was intended for service up and down the River Seine; it seems a fair bet that he never crossed the Channel again.

The 1816 crossing was a one-off affair: it was not until the spring of 1821 that a regular service began from Dover to Calais. The first sea-going steamship was the 88-ton *Rob Roy,* built in Dumbarton in 1818 and first used on a triangular service between Dublin and Belfast and Greenock on the Clyde. This, however, showed little profit and her owners, David Napier Ltd, sold her to a Dover businessman, John Boyd. For the next three summers the *Rob Roy* sailed on a regular run between Dover and Calais, taking around two hours 45 minutes in calm weather. Mr Boyd then sold her to the French Government.

In these early days few passengers could be persuaded to buy a ticket because steamships frequently broke down and the danger of a boiler explosion was considerable. However the introduction of iron plates to strengthen the hull, and improvements in boiler design, soon made the short Channel crossing safe, reliable and surprisingly fast. By 1887, for example, when the steamship *Empress* came into service, the passage could be made in little more than 50 minutes, measured harbour mouth to harbour mouth.

Embarking and disembarking passengers, however, was a slow and inefficient affair, and the hoist continued to play a key part in vehicular cross-Channel traffic for the best part of a century. In 1909, a batch of pioneer motorists and their cars were shipped across the Channel for the first time; although at Calais a heavy-handed crane driver put down one of the vehicles with undue vigour and damaged its crankshaft.

### Captain Townsend – pioneer
The first ship to offer a specialised service for motorists was the *Artificer,* a redundant minesweeper bought for a song in 1928 by the enterprising Captain Stuart Townsend, a step which led to the creation of the present-day Townsend Thoresen company. Captain Townsend began modestly

*A London–Paris train being shunted on to the ferry at Dover in 1936*

*The SRN1 – the first hovercraft to cross the Channel*

enough, taking just 15 cars between Dover and Calais, and using a dockside crane to lift them on and off his ship.

In those days only a true motoring fanatic would have braved a trip in the *Artificer* when her facilities were spartan, to say the least. For the following year rail travel reached its luxurious pinnacle with an all-Pullman service between London and Brussels. The old Southern Railway Company (the concept of British Rail was far in the future) built and brought into service the steamship *Canterbury,* which was reserved exclusively for Golden Arrow passengers who had travelled by train between Victoria and Dover. On the other side of the Channel, where the Golden Arrow naturally became the Flèche d'Or, another Pullman express awaited the arrival of the *Canterbury* to whisk its passengers on to Brussels.

## RO–RO

The Southern Railway did however take note of Captain Townsend's increasingly profitable activity sufficiently to introduce their own car ferry, the *Autocarrier,* in the summer of 1930. But the first ferry with a roll-on roll-off section specially for cars was not built until 1934, in anticipation of the Night Ferry service by which passengers could join the train at Victoria, be safely tucked in for the night, and wake up the following morning on the outskirts of Brussels or Paris. Those really rich travellers who wanted to take their cars, and presumably their chauffeurs, could store the vehicles above the train deck with anchor points to keep the wheels firmly in position. At any rate, by 1936 it was possible to take one's car all the way from London to Paris on the Night Ferry by way of Dover and Dunkerque. It was the forerunner of motorail, but sadly, a journey that is no longer possible.

## Purpose-built

It was not until the early fifties that special ramps were built at the Eastern Docks for the benefit of motorists, following the introduction by British Rail of the first completely purpose-built car ferry, the *Lord Warden,* which began operations on the Calais route on June 17, 1952. But the Townsend company did not lag behind for long. In 1962 they introduced a new ferry class, beginning with *Free Enterprise I*, and six years later went into partnership with the Norwegian operator, Thoresen.

British Rail responded by cementing their partnership with, on routes out of Dover, French Railways (SNCF) and the Belgian Maritime Authority (RMT), adopting a common tariff and complimentary timetable. The sale of Sealink UK in 1984 to Sea Containers Ltd., owners of the Orient Express, and the establishment of a new company called British Ferries Ltd, has done nothing to affect this tri-partisan agreement.

## P&O joins in

Sealink and Townsend Thoresen had the market much their own way until 1976, when a third shipping company began to operate from Dover to Boulogne.

This was P & O, plausibly credited with giving a new word to the English language. The most agreeable way to travel on their liners to India avoiding the extreme heat of the sun was with a cabin on the port side of the ship on the outward journey, and on the starboard side on the return. Tickets were stamped with the abbreviation for Port Out, Starboard Home, P.O.S.H., so that 'posh' became jargon for up-market travel, then up-market everything.

However P & O found themselves increasingly squeezed in the fiercely competitive ferry operations of the Channel. They were unable to generate sufficient profit to replace their ageing fleet and early in 1985 they sold out to European Ferries – owners of Townsend Thoresen. Curiously, Townsend had sailed the route to Boulogne for a single summer before concentrating on Calais. Now returning to Boulogne cost them £12.5 million, a far cry from the days when Captain Townsend risked the wrath of his bank manager by replacing a converted minesweeper with . . . a converted frigate.

## Hovercraft

Townsend's pioneering spirit extended in the early 1960s to a revolutionary new concept: the hovercraft. For a trial season,

weather permitting, they operated a small craft that took 35 passengers to France. However much bigger, car-carrying hovercraft were not long delayed. On August 1 1968 the British Rail Seaspeed hovercraft *Princess Margaret* ran for the first time between Dover and Boulogne. The new craft, an SR–N4 Mountbatten Class ACV, weighed 168 tons and was powered by four Bristol Siddeley Marine Proteus gasturbine engines. It was licensed to carry 609 passengers, or 254 passengers and 30 cars.

In October 1981 a merger took place between Seaspeed and the Swedish-owned Hoverlloyd to form Hoverspeed, who operate all the Hovercraft services out of Dover.

The hovercraft was the brainchild of Christopher Cockerell, an electronics engineer and amateur boat-builder in Suffolk, who in 1954 used an empty tin of Heinz baked beans, another empty, but slightly larger, tin of Lyons coffee, and a vacuum cleaner of doubtful identity to prove his theory of the 'annular jet'. Cockerell switched the vacuum cleaner to blow rather than suck, and measured on his kitchen scales the strength of the thin stream of air thrust downwards between the outer wall of the smaller tin, and the inner wall of the larger. The jet of air was trebled in strength by being squeezed between the tins, and the hovercraft principle was confirmed in practice.

Sir Christopher Cockerell, as he later became, patented his invention in 1955. However it took another 13 years to perfect a hovercraft that could be certain to operate continuously in all but the most turbulent conditions of the English Channel. A further decade elapsed before a hydrofoil began to link Ostende with the United Kingdom, at first travelling up the Thames to the Port of London, but now on the shorter and consequently much more reliable route to Dover. And yet a hydrofoil had been first built by the Comte de Lambert, and tested on the Seine, as long ago as 1897, showing that passenger transport can take a long time to be transformed from dream to reality.

# The Crossing

Ships and costs compared; routes across the world's busiest waterway

*Two ferries pass each other off Calais*

The most contented cross-Channel traveller is the one who does his homework the most thoroughly. For while there is a superficial similarity between the range of services offered, it is the differences that may prove vital in determining the success, or disappointment, of your Continental excursion.

Apart from its increasingly fast road links with the rest of the United Kingdom, the real advantage of Dover is the variety of routes and means of transportation it offers across the Channel:

**To France**

| Calais | 21 miles | Ferry and hovercraft |
| Boulogne | 25 miles | Ferry and hovercraft |
| Dunkerque | 40 miles | Ferry |

**To Belgium**

| Ostende | 62 miles | Ferry and jetfoil |
| Zeebrugge | 77 miles | Ferry |

| Sailing times from Dover | | | | |
|---|---|---|---|---|
| | Sealink | Townsend | Hoverspeed | Jetfoil |
| Calais | 1 hr 30 min | 1 hr 15 min | 35 min | – |
| Boulogne | 1 hr 45 min | 1 hr 40 min | 40 min | – |
| Dunkerque | 2 hr 20 min | – | – | – |
| Ostende | 3 hr 45 min | – | – | 1 hr 40 min |
| Zeebrugge | – | 4 hr 15 min | – | – |

On a peak summer's day more than 100 ferry or hovercraft sailings leave Dover, lending strength to the Dover Harbour Board's undertaking that a motorist arriving without a reservation, or too late for the original booking, will be well looked after. Provided the motorist is prepared, if necessary, to accept another destination port, the DHB promise to have him or her under way within three hours of their intended departure time.

## Speed

If the speed of your arrival in Belgium or France is your priority, it is beyond dispute that the quickest way to cross the Channel is by hovercraft, 35 minutes from Dover to Calais and 40 minutes to Boulogne (see box). The operators, Hoverspeed, also claim a further advantage in the time it takes to load and unload. They say that even their largest craft, which can take up to 52 cars and more than 400 passengers, takes only ten minutes to embark and even less to disembark. As a result, a carload of passengers can normally be on their way out of Calais one hour and a quarter after checking in at Dover.

This is an impressive statistic, but it overlooks one vital point. For many motorists, Dover represents a staging point on a long journey with a good deal of travelling in the UK itself. In such circumstances, the opportunity to have a leisurely meal and perhaps even a rest may prove particularly welcome. On the Hoverspeed services, passengers are virtually confined to their seats, where they will be served drinks and offered a selection of duty-free goods; but any substantial meal or close look at a wide range of duty-free goods has to be done

before departure, extending the journey time accordingly.

On the ferry routes, a direct comparison is possible between Sealink British Ferries and Townsend Thoresen. On Townsend, the crossing to Calais takes 1 hour 15 minutes; Sealink do the same passage in 1½ hours. A difference of 15 minutes is not really of great significance except on those odd occasions when perhaps at the height of the season, the berths at Calais or Dover are under pressure. On some sailings, a Townsend ship might leave Calais behind its Sealink rival and still slip into Dover first.

All Townsend Thoresen sailings are from Dover's Eastern Docks, where the minimum check-in time is the same as for the hovercraft, 30 minutes before departure. However some Sealink sailings to Calais and Ostende, and all sailings to Dunkerque, go from the Western Docks, where the minimum check in time is 45 minutes, 15 minutes longer. On the Ostende route the usual journey time is 3¾ hours, but in order to make the schedules more convenient, some sailings take 4¼ hours – helpful perhaps during the night if you are trying to snatch a few hours sleep, irritating during the day if you are anxious to press on to your destination.

However the Jetfoil, for foot passengers only, takes just 1 hour 40 minutes to Ostende from Dover, less than half the time of the fastest ferry.

## Eating on board

On the Calais route, you might expect Townsend to offer only a self-service restaurant and Sealink, with extra time at sea, to be able to provide a waiter service.

| Which ship goes where | | | |
|---|---|---|---|
| **Ferries** | | | |
| **Dover-Calais** | *Company* | *Passengers* | *Cars* |
| St Anselm | Sealink British Ferries | 1400 | 310 |
| St Christopher | Sealink British Ferries | 1400 | 310 |
| Côte d'Azur | Sealink SNCF | 1600 | 330 |
| Champs Elysées | Sealink SNCF† | 1800 | 330 |
| Spirit of Free Enterprise | Townsend Thoresen | 1300 | 350 |
| Herald of Free Enterprise | Townsend Thoresen | 1300 | 350 |
| Pride of Free Enterprise | Townsend Thoresen | 1300 | 350 |
| **Dover-Dunkerque** | | | |
| St Eloi | Sealink SNCF* | 1000 | 164 |
| **Dover-Boulogne** | | | |
| Tiger | Townsend Thoresen | 1004 | 160 |
| Panther | Townsend Thoresen | 1004 | 160 |
| **Dover-Ostende** | | | |
| Prins Phillippe | Sealink RTM | 1302 | 248 |
| Prince Laurent | Sealink RTM | 1302 | 170 |
| Prinses Paola | Sealink RTM | 1700 | ** |
| Prins Albert | Sealink RTM | 1400 | 236 |
| Princesse Marie Christine | Sealink RTM | 1200 | 276 |
| Reine Astrid | Sealink RTM | 1200 | 500 |
| Stena Nordica | Sealink RTM* | 1500 | 425 |
| St David | Sealink British Ferries | 1000 | 306 |
| **Dover-Zeebrugge** | | | |
| Free Enterprise VI | Townsend Thoresen | 1200 | 350 |
| Free Enterprise VII | Townsend Thoresen | 1200 | 350 |
| Free Enterprise VIII | Townsend Thoresen | 1200 | 350 |
| | | | |
| **Hovercraft** | | | |
| **Dover-Calais/Boulogne** | | | |
| Princess Anne | Hoverspeed | 424 | 52 |
| Princess Margaret | Hoverspeed | 424 | 52 |
| Swift | Hoverspeed | 278 | 32 |
| Sure | Hoverspeed | 278 | 32 |
| Prince of Wales | Hoverspeed | 278 | 32 |
| Sir Christopher | Hoverspeed | 278 | 32 |
| †also operates Dover-Boulogne | *on charter | **freight only | |

## Guide to ferry schedules

### Sealink British Ferries

| Dover–Calais | Calais–Dover |
| --- | --- |
| *Eastern and Western Docks* | |
| *0030 DE* sp | **0100 DE** |
| **0100 DE** s, a & w | **0300 DE** |
| **0300 DE** | **0500 DE** |
| **0500 DE** | **0630 DE** |
| **0630 DE** | **0745 DE** |
| **0915 DE** | **0845 DE** |
| **1015 DE** n | **1000 DE** |
| **1130 DE** | 1100 DW |
| 1240 DW | **1130 DE** |
| **1300 DE** | **1330 DE** |
| **1550 DE** | **1445 DE** n |
| **1630 DE** n | **1500 DW** |
| **1630 DW** | **1700 DE** |
| **1845 DE** | 1715 DW |
| 1930 DW | **1845 DE** |
| **2015 DE** | **2000 DE** n |
| **2130 DE** | **2100 DE** |
| **2300 DE** | **2230 DE** |

| Dover–Boulogne | Boulogne–Dover |
| --- | --- |
| *Eastern Docks–Wed and Sat only* | |
| **1015** | **1430** |
| **1630** | **2000** |

| Dover–Dunkerque | Dunkerque–Dover |
| --- | --- |
| *Western Docks* | |
| **0720** | **0400** |
| **1510** | **1150** |
| **2320** | **2000** |

| Dover–Ostende | Ostende–Dover |
| --- | --- |
| *Eastern and Western Docks* | |
| **0100 DE** | **0001 DE** |
| **0400 DE** | *0130 DW* sp |
| **0700 DE** | **0200 DW** |
| 1000 DE | **0500 DE** |
| **1115 DW** | **0700 DW** |
| 1300 DE | **0830 DE** |
| *1515 DW* sp, a & w | *1005 DW* sp, a & w |
| 1600 DE | 1200 DE |
| *1815 DW* sp | *1350 DW* a |
| **1900 DE** | *1400 DW* sp |
| 2200 DE | **1445 DE** |
| *2300 DW* sp | **1700 DE** |
| 2330 DW | *1830 DW* sp & a |
| | **2030 DE** |

### Jetfoil

*Jetfoil Terminal–Western Docks*

| Dover–Ostende | Ostende–Dover |
| --- | --- |
| *0825* s | 0710 s |
| **1005** | **0830** |
| **1320** | **1155** |
| **1525** | **1350** |
| **1750** | **1635** |
| **2050** | **1930** |

**Note**
Ferry schedules are subject to alteration and cancellation.
All times given are local times.
Because of the difference in summer time between the Continent and the UK, ferry times on some services may be changed between 29 September and 27 October.

**Key**
| | |
| --- | --- |
| **bold** | daily for most of the year |
| roman | summer service |
| *italics* | service for shorter periods |
| w | winter |
| sp | spring |
| s | summer |
| a | autumn |
| we | weekends |
| n | not Wed or Sat |
| DE | Eastern Docks |
| DW | Western Docks |

| Townsend Thoresen | | Hoverspeed | |
|---|---|---|---|
| **Dover–Calais** | **Calais–Dover** | **Dover–Calais** | **Calais–Dover** |
| *Eastern Docks* | | *Hoverport, Western Docks* | |
| 0200 | 0015 | 0600 s | *0800* s |
| *0300* w | *0130* w | *0630* s | 0830 s |
| 0400 | 0200 | 0700 | 0900 |
| **0600** | *0300* sp | *0730* s | *0930* s |
| 0730 | 0400 | **0800** | **1000** |
| **0900** | *0430* w | 0900+we | 1100+we |
| **1030** | 0600 | *0940* s | *1130* a |
| 1200 | **0730** | 1030 | *1140* s |
| *1300* w | **0915** | 1100 | 1230 |
| 1330 | 1045 | *1130* w | |
| **1500** | *1115* sp | 1140 | 1300 |
| 1630 | *1200* w | 1230 | |
| *1730* w | 1215 | 1340 | 1340 |
| 1800 | **1345** | *1400* w | 1430 |
| **1930** | 1515 | 1420 | *1440* a |
| 2100 | *1545* sp | *1440* s & we | 1540 |
| *2200* w | *1615* w | *1540* s | *1600* a |
| 2230 | 1645 | *1600* w & we | 1620 |
| **2359** | *1745* sp | 1630 | *1630* w |
| | **1815** | 1730 | *1640* s & we |
| | 1945 | 1830 | *1740* s |
| | *2045* w | *1930* s | *1800* a & we |
| | 2115 | | 1830 |
| | **2245** | | 1930 |
| | | | 2030 |
| | | | 2130 |

| Dover–Boulogne | Boulogne–Dover |
|---|---|
| *Eastern Docks* | |
| *All services one hour later in winter* | |
| 0200 | **0300** |
| **0500** | **0600** |
| **0800** | **0900** |
| **1100** | **1200** |
| **1400** | **1500** |
| **1700** | **1800** |
| **2000** | **2100** |
| **2300** | **2359** |

| Dover–Boulogne | Boulogne–Dover |
|---|---|
| *Hoverport, Western Docks* | |
| 0830 | |
| 1000 | 1030 |
| 1210 | 1205 |
| 1310 | 1405 |
| 1510 | 1505 |
| *1610* a | 1705+a |
| *1810* s | *2005* s |

| Dover–Zeebrugge | Zeebrugge–Dover |
|---|---|
| *Eastern Docks* | |
| **0530** | **0100** |
| **0830** | **0400** |
| **1130** | **0700** |
| **1730** | **1300** |
| **2030** | **1600** |
| **2330** | **1900** |

**Key**
| | | | |
|---|---|---|---|
| **bold** | daily for most of the year | | |
| roman | summer service | | |
| *italics* | service for shorter periods | | |
| w | winter | we | weekends |
| sp | spring | n | not Wed or Sat |
| s | summer | DE | Eastern Docks |
| a | autumn | DW | Western Docks |

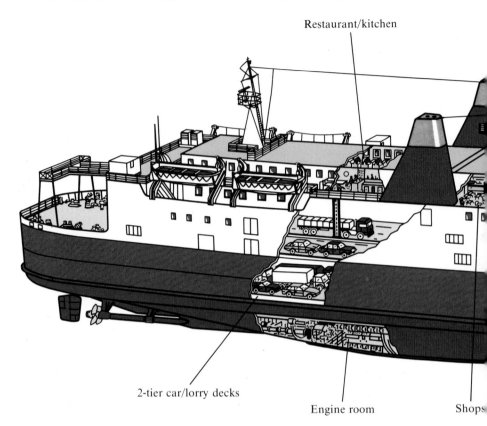

Restaurant/kitchen

2-tier car/lorry decks

Engine room

Shops

In fact it is the other way round, or rather, Townsend offers both, and Sealink self-service only. These restaurants are not particularly large, and on busy days it is essential to stake your claim to a table the moment you drive on to the ship, if necessary by sending one of your party on ahead. A great advantage of these restaurants is that however busy the ship may be on peak summer crossings, you remain cocooned from the crowds in a separate area.

Even if you are not using the restaurant, eating first is a sound principle, as there may be very few passengers waiting at the start of the voyage, and the food will undoubtedly be at its best.

On the longer routes, Sealink provide only self-service to Dunkerque; but all the Sealink sailings to Ostende, and the Town-send services to Zeebrugge, offer a choice between self and waiter service. The longer Townsend sailings also provide films in a special cinema or on video. All the ships on all the routes out of Dover provide duty-free and other shops, a bar or bars with duty-free prices, and a bureau de change. An increasing number of ships also offer special facilities for mothers with babies, and for children.

### Newest

If your priority is to sail on the newest ferries on a Dover route (and Dover has the pick of the ferries operated by all the companies), then Sealink has the most recent additions to its fleet. The French Railways ship *Champs Elysées,* was the latest to come into service, on October 4, 1984. She is licensed to carry 1800 passen-

*The layout of a modern ferry*

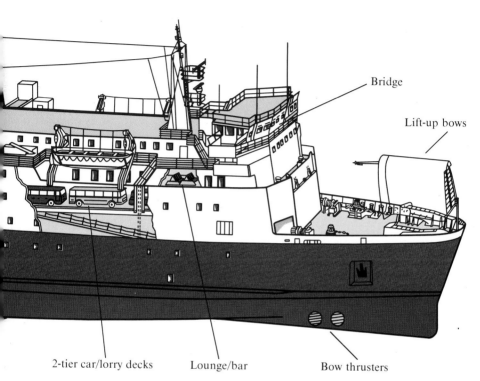

2-tier car/lorry decks          Lounge/bar          Bow thrusters

Bridge

Lift-up bows

gers, more than any other ship on a Dover route.

The two new Sealink British Ferries ships, *St Anselm* amd *St Christopher,* and the other new French Railways ship, *Côte d'Azur,* are of the same generation as the three ultra-modern Townsend Thoresen ferries on the Dover-Calais run, the *Spirit, Herald* and *Pride of Free Enterprise.* If the Sealink ships can carry the most passengers, between 1400 and 1800, the rebuilt Townsend older *Free Enterprise* fleet could carry the most cars – over 500 cars on each sailing.

## Prices

While destination, crossing time, and both new and extensive facilities can influence your choice, for most travellers the price of the trip remains of paramount import-

ance. A few years back there seemed to be a gentleman's agreement on fares and fare structure, to such an extent that tickets were readily interchangeable between the companies; this is no longer the case.    No book can offer an infallible analysis of the most economic method of travel for every possible combination of cars, passengers and dates. There are, however, some general points to consider:–

If you book direct with the ferry company, it is extremely unlikely that they will draw your attention to a lower fare on offer from a competitor;

If you book through an agent, the amount of commission he earns is usually much less than, for example, on a standard package tour that includes hotels as well as the means of travel. Human nature being what it is, he or his staff will be prepared to devote only a limited time to your particular requirements. Remember, paradoxically, the more money they save you, the less they actually earn;

The highest fares are charged in periods when operators are confident that they can fill their ferries or hovercraft without difficulty – in other words, out of Dover on a Friday afternoon or Saturday morning during a school holiday period. To keep down the cost, consider travelling late at night, early in the morning, midweek, or out of school holidays – by law, you are entitled to take children away from school for two weeks in term time each year, if you are satisfied it will not adversely affect their work;

Most of the companies offer five day and 60-hour excursions at greatly reduced rates. Your time limit is calculated from your arrival abroad, and contrary to some people's impression, you do not have to be back in the UK within that time limit, or even on board the return sailing. Simply taking the next sailing after the time limit will suffice – which can extend your time allowance considerably;

On most crossings to Ostende and Zeebrugge, cabins are available that can save you a night's hotel accommodation on one or other side of the Channel. Cabins are particularly cheap on day sailings, but still an excellent means of keeping fresh for the journey ahead;

You are not obliged to book both halves of your trip (other than excursion fares) with the same company. It may well be cheaper to use a different operator for each sailing.

So before you book, obtain a brochure containing the current prices from each operator and satisfy yourself that you really have worked out the best possible deal. A few minutes' effort can result in a substantial saving, and make all the difference to the overall price of your holiday.

## The crew at work

Paradoxical though it may seem, when a ship is in port, the crew may well work at their hardest. At peak periods the turnaround from one sailing to the next into or out of Dover is so rapid that there is barely time to replenish stocks of food, drink and duty-free goods. 'It's quite frantic some days,' said a purser who has been working on these routes for nearly 20 years. 'Some-

*The car deck*

times we barely have time to unplug the vacuum cleaners before the next load of passengers arrive. The lounges can be spotless as we leave, but when I go by during the crossing, some horrible little boy will somehow have managed to collect chips, ice cream and cola into one incredibly sticky mess. Whatever strengths the British may have, being tidy isn't one of them.'

One of the ship's officers is in charge of loading the vehicles, which, however quiet the crossing, are always placed just as close as they can be to the car in front. 'Two reasons for that', according to one senior officer. 'First, we never quite know when a lot of people are going to arrive at the last minute. They'd be the first to complain, and quite rightly, if we didn't have room for them on board because we had left two feet between virtually every car. The second reason is one of safety. We ask all drivers to park with the handbrake on and in gear, just in case the ship does start moving about. There's nearly always someone who forgets, and usually it's the owner who's made his car nearly as impregnable as Fort Knox. And while we're finding him, we certainly don't want his car running backwards and forwards in plenty of space like a battering ram.'

For safety reasons, too, all heavy objects on the passenger decks are fixed to the wall or the deck, and watertight doors make it possible for every ferry to be divided into compartments. 'We have to be prepared for the worst, for any eventuality, because that is one way of making almost certain that there never will be a real emergency,' said one senior captain.

'Passengers sometimes ask why we don't have boat drill. The answer is, of course, that we have so many passengers in the course of an average day, if we had a drill on every sailing, the crew would be exhausted, and the passengers would never get a meal or their duty-free! However we do have special drill for the crew at regular intervals, to make sure that they know what to do. The truth of the matter, though, is that we are far more likely to be involved in rescuing someone else than to need rescuing ourselves.'

## World's busiest waterway

The English Channel, and the Dover Strait in particular, is easily the busiest waterway in the world. More than 600 ships pass through or backwards and forwards daily. The Channel is now run like a huge motorway, with east-west traffic divided into separate lanes (see chart pp. 44–5). Looking out from Dover, you come first to what is known as the English inshore traffic zone in which ships can travel in more or less any direction. Next is the south-west shipping lane, in which ships passing from the North Sea to the Bay of Biscay are required to travel south-west, that is from left to right. Then comes a central zone, closed to through traffic, but open to fisherman. Next is the north-east lane, in which ships proceeding from the Bay of Biscay towards the North Sea are required to sail north-east, that is, from right to left. Finally there is a French equivalent of the inshore traffic zone on their side of the Channel. Very large ships have to notify their intention to enter the Strait in advance, and to keep to a narrow channel known as the deep water route.

Ferries and hovercraft are obliged to cross the Channel at approximately right-angles to these shipping lanes. Indeed, any ship crossing the Strait or joining or leaving the lanes is supposed to do so on a course as close to a right-angle as possible. But while it is now very rare for a ship to ignore the lane direction altogether, some still do contravene this joining regulation, either through carelessness or in order to steer a dangerous short-cut, to save time and fuel.

### Coastguards

The Channel policemen, if you like, are the Dover Coastguard. Their radar station, known as the Langdon Battery, is perched high on the cliffs overlooking Dover's Eastern Docks. In peak periods the radar screen may have as many as 150 ships in view. In order to identify precisely ships that sail off-course, the coastguards employ a spotter plane based at Lydd Airport in Kent. The coastguard gives the vessel's precise co-ordinates, and the plane

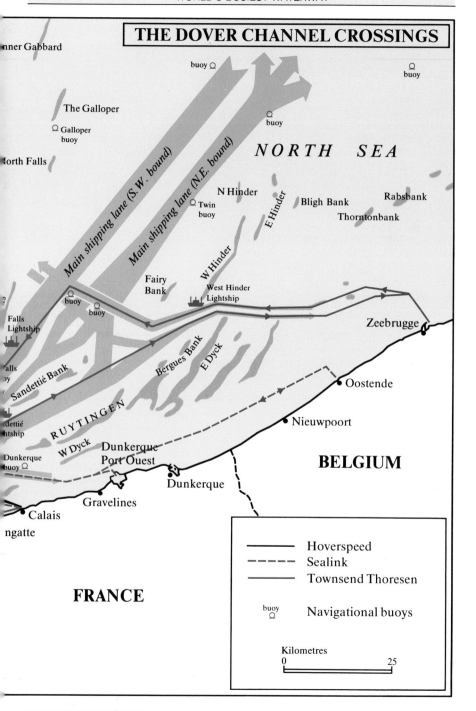

# THE DOVER CHANNEL CROSSINGS

nner Gabbard

buoy ○

○
buoy

The Galloper

○ Galloper
buoy

*NORTH   SEA*

lorth Falls

*Main shipping lane (S.W. bound)*

*Main shipping lane (N.E. bound)*

buoy
○

N Hinder

○ Twin
buoy

E Hinder

Bligh Bank

Rabsbank

Thorntonbank

W Hinder

Fairy
Bank

West Hinder
⊥⊥⊥ Lightship

○
buoy

○
buoy

Falls
Lightship
⊥⊥⊥

Zeebrugge

Bergues Bank

E Dyck

alls
oy

Sandettié Bank

RUYTINGEN

Oostende

dettié
htship

W Dyck

Nieuwpoort

Dunkerque ○
buoy

Dunkerque
Port Ouest

Dunkerque

**BELGIUM**

Gravelines

• Calais

ngatte

**FRANCE**

| | Hoverspeed |
|---|---|
| ------- | Sealink |
| | Townsend Thoresen |

buoy
○   Navigational buoys

Kilometres
0               25

*On the bridge*

will fly over it at low level to pick out its name and place of registration.

What happens next depends on the country in which the ship is registered. Some countries will prosecute masters found flagrantly ignoring the rules of the sea, and those found guilty face heavy fines and even suspension. Others, however, will do little or nothing.

The coastguard may try to warn ships that they are breaking the rules but as there is no uniform international requirements for them to be tuned even to an emergency channel, such attempts are often unsuccessful. Even when they are listening, some ships may be tempted not to reply in the hope that they will not be identified.

### Crossing by radar

Fortunately, the sophisticated electronic equipment on board almost all the modern ferries has made life much simpler for the captain. Really bad weather in the Channel is actually extremely rare, but radar, linked to a computer, makes it possible for schedules to be maintained, however poor the visibility. The computer plots the course of other vessels in the vicinity, assessing and constantly re-assessing their course and speed and providing the ferry captain with a course of his own that is guaranteed to keep the ships a safe distance apart.

Most passengers still feel secure in the knowledge that on the bridge is a master of enormous experience and instinctive seamanship that can occasionally be needed for the most difficult manoeuvre, the final approach into port. Many of the most modern ships possess bow thrusters that enable these ferries, despite their size, to turn on the proverbial sixpence or stop in virtually their own length; and the Dover Harbour Board owns two tugs, which are available to help if needed in adverse conditions.

Yet the future offers even more sophisticated technology for those dozen or so days each year when the weather makes life difficult for the ferry captain. A fully-automated pilot system has been developed to bring ships easily into port. Known as Vagin (Vehicle Automatic Guidance and Integrated Navigation), it uses details of the ship's characteristics, in particular sea conditions, together with information from its navigation system. From this the on-board computer calculates the ship's position and automatically locks on to the most favourable route into port, using data on the port approaches stored in the computer's memory. As the captain said with a smile, 'It won't be long before *we're* landing in fog at Heathrow too.'

# You're there!

## Off the ship, through the formalities and away you go

*Modern ramps make disembarking easy*

The hovercraft does have two particular, though not particularly significant, advantages over the ferry when you come to disembark. Firstly, it is almost impossible actually to become lost on a hovercraft, or at any rate to lose your car, or the rest of the family, or both: this is all too easy on a ferry. Secondly, the hovercraft does not carry lorries, which, despite the most determined efforts of the ferry companies, still occasionally persist in warming up their engines on the car decks and thereby giving the motorists a whiff of noxious fumes.

It follows that motorists using ferries need to strike a fine balance between returning to their vehicles too early, that is at the moment the announcement is made asking them to do so, and risking claustrophobia, or suffocation or both; and returning so late that cars have already begun to disembark, and there is a queue of irate fellow drivers waiting for them to move.

As, by and large, on the new 'through' ferries, motorists can expect to leave the ship in the order of priority determined by their arrival at the quayside in Dover, it is not too difficult to work out that you should hurry if you were among the first to go aboard, and be a little more leisurely if you were among the late arrivals. However it is essential to remember on which deck and which side of the ship you left your car, because if you make a mistake, you could find yourself struggling against a tide of humanity that possesses a better idea where their cars are located. Townsend Thoresen ferries have devised a series of animal symbols to make identifying the correct deck a simple task. And the children can help, too.

In the few minutes available before you are given a signal to start your engine and drive off the ship, there is usually time to prepare yourself for the official checks on the far side of the Channel. On nearly every occasion, these will be cursory and barely slow you down; but in extremely rare circumstances, perhaps the result of a visit from some prominent official from Paris or Brussels, a more rigorous inspection will be made. You may be asked to produce:

Your passport, and those of everyone travelling with you;
The registration document of your car;
Documentary evidence that the car is insured;
Items on which duty should be paid.

You will not be asked to produce your ferry ticket again until the return journey.

At some ports, immigration and customs checks may be some way from the point of disembarkation, but officials will be on hand to point you in the right direction. If you have to queue, and have a choice of lanes, where possible avoid stopping behind a French car (if you are entering France) or a Belgian car (if you are entering Belgium), as customs checks on them may be much more vigorous, and at some checkpoints it is not always easy to drive around a car delayed in front. Coaches, too, represent a possible delay, as passengers may be asked to leave the coach for individual passport checks.

**Passports and customs**

Passport control comes first, and normally represents no difficulty, as French officials are aware of the close scrutiny made by British officials back in Dover. It is quite common for vehicles to be waved on without any kind of passport inspection, and the same may apply when a motorist is leaving France.

Customs officials may be even less in evidence. If the officials seem firmly closeted in their office, and show no inclination to inspect either you or your vehicle, drive on at a modest pace.

If you are stopped, you will probably be asked if you have anything to declare. For each person aged 15 or over, the following can be imported without duty, if purchased on board ship:-

|  | Belgium | France |
|---|---|---|
| Cigarettes *or* | 300 | 200 |
| Cigars | 75 | 50 |
| Spirits | 1½ litres | 1 litre |
| Perfume | 75g | 50g |

Personal effects are unlikely to be subject to close scrutiny, except cameras (you are allowed two, each with ten rolls of film) and portable TV sets, specifically excluded from duty if you intend to re-export it from France, but not specifically excluded from duty in Belgium. A full tank of petrol is permitted in both France and Belgium without duty being imposed.

The Belgian authorities are more likely to ask for the vehicle registration document, and, unless this shows you to be the owner, they may ask to see a letter from the owner or from the car hire company.

*Driving on the right soon becomes simple*

In both countries you may be asked to provide some evidence of insurance for the car. Strictly speaking, a UK insurance certificate shows that you have the minimum insurance required to drive in the rest of the European Community, but it is what it says, the barest minimum – no cover for your own car, yourself or your passengers, even if you have comprehensive insurance in the UK. The increasingly common British insurance certificate that does not specify the vehicles covered, can also lead to difficulties on the Continent. A Green Card is still the most sensible precaution for any motoring trip abroad (see p.11).

### Driving on the right

A motorist driving on the right for the first time, or even for the first time within a year, may feel that he or she has enough to contend with. In reality, the experience is far more agreeable than the anticipation.

Drivers soon grow used to the differences. There are, however, a few points to watch:

Resist the temptation to drive too close to the verges or pavements simply because you are now sitting on that side of the road and can judge the distance more accurately. Cyclists are used to being given a wide berth, and may react sharply to cars that seem to pass them too closely;

If you stop at a petrol station, a shop or a café, other things being equal try to choose one on the right-hand side of the road, as this will minimise the risk of your forgetting where you are and driving off on the left-hand side;

Overtaking can be a problem because, in order to see if the road is clear yourself, you would have to swing your car out into the oncoming lane. Planning your journey so that from the very start you have an alert front-seat passenger with good judgement is therefore essential: this is no seat for a kamikaze teenager or a myopic aunt;

| British Gallons/Litres | | | |
|---|---|---|---|
| litres | gallons | gallons | litres |
| 1 | 0.22 | 1 | 4.54 |
| 2 | 0.44 | 2 | 9.09 |
| 3 | 0.66 | 3 | 13.63 |
| 4 | 0.88 | 4 | 18.18 |
| 5 | 1.10 | 5 | 22.73 |
| 10 | 2.20 | 6 | 27.27 |
| 20 | 4.40 | 7 | 31.82 |
| 30 | 6.60 | 8 | 36.36 |
| 40 | 8.80 | 9 | 40.91 |
| 50 | 11.00 | 10 | 45.46 |
| 100 | 22.00 | 20 | 90.92 |

| Tyre pressures | |
|---|---|
| Pounds per square inch | kilogrammes per square centimetre |
| 18 | 1.26 |
| 20 | 1.40 |
| 22 | 1.54 |
| 24 | 1.68 |
| 26 | 1.83 |
| 28 | 1.96 |
| 30 | 2.10 |
| 32 | 2.24 |
| 36 | 2.52 |
| 40 | 2.80 |

Turning left can be equally difficult because you are in effect carrying out the most difficult manoeuvre on a British road – turning right – with everything reversed: the key is to take up a good position in the centre of the road, fix in your mind where your car should be after the manoeuvre is completed, and pick your moment to turn.

**Priorité à droite**
Priority to the right means what it says: giving way to traffic coming from your right. In theory it should only apply to roads of equal status or in towns, but the more elderly the driver of any car, the more likely he is to shoot out in front of you with barely a glance. In France, and

| Miles/Kilometres | | |
|---|---|---|
| miles or km | miles | km |
| 1 | 0.621 | 1.609 |
| 2 | 1.242 | 3.218 |
| 3 | 1.864 | 4.827 |
| 4 | 2.485 | 6.437 |
| 5 | 3.107 | 8.046 |
| 6 | 3.728 | 9.655 |
| 7 | 4.350 | 11.265 |
| 8 | 4.971 | 12.874 |
| 9 | 5.592 | 14.483 |
| 10 | 6.211 | 16.093 |
| 20 | 12.428 | 32.186 |
| 25 | 15.535 | 40.232 |
| 50 | 31.070 | 80.465 |
| 100 | 62.136 | 160.930 |
| 200 | 124.272 | 321.860 |
| 300 | 186.408 | 482.790 |

in West Germany should you be going there, this priority rule does not normally apply to roundabouts, where traffic already on them still has right of way. However in France, where this rule was introduced in May 1984, there are still some roundabouts under the control of local authorities who have simply ignored the advice of central government. The only advice when approaching a French roundabout is therefore to be prepared for any eventuality.

The routes around the five Continental ports served by Dover – Boulogne, Calais, Dunkerque, Ostende and Zeebrugge – do give the inexperienced driver ample opportunity to adjust to the unfamiliar motoring conditions. They are also the simplest to follow if you intend to join one of the major motorways in Belgium or France. However it must also be said that they add considerably to the journey, particularly at Calais and Boulogne, and may themselves be congested, especially in the summer.

Other than during the morning and early evening (later than in the UK, though) rush hours from Monday to Friday, or mid morning on Saturdays, the much shorter route through the centre of the ports can be as quick, and certainly a more interesting experience. Further, signposting in the centre of Continental towns is far superior to that in the United Kingdom, where a motorist can find himself deserted by signposts at a critical moment.

*Opposite: through routes from ferry terminals and hoverports in Boulogne and Calais*

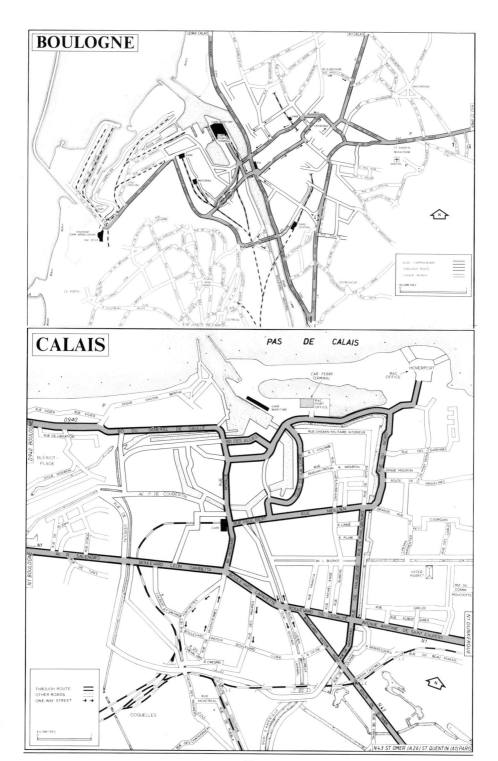

# BOULOGNE

# CALAIS

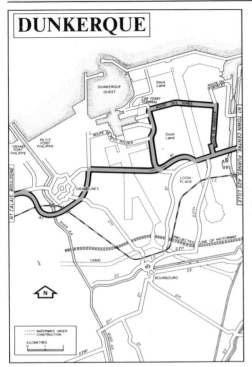

*Left: Dunkerque port is a few miles west of Dunkerque itself which is reached along the N 1, the road which also takes you to the motorway network*

*Opposite: the major routes round and from Bruges as well as those from the port of Zeebrugge*

*Below: through routes from the ferry terminal in Ostende*

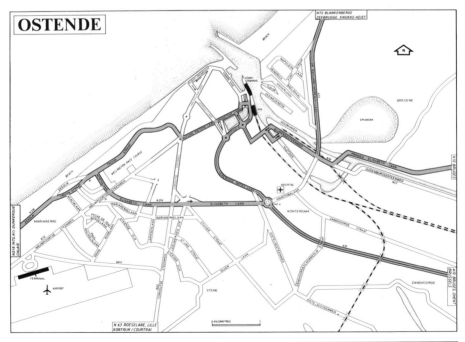

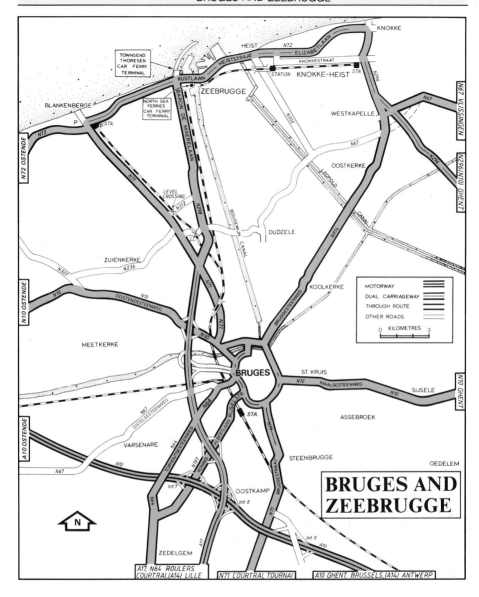

## The ports

Roads shown in green are the through routes which lead to the major roads. Railway stations, car ferry terminals and hoverports are also shown but only some other roads.

Maps showing the links from the ports to the motorway network are on page 125.

Street maps, showing the central areas of each town are in the chapter Sur le Continent as follows:

# It's foreign

## Not only the language is different, the food, drink and way of life is too

*In the Place du Tertre, Montmartre, Paris*

### Cafés

The French go to cafés almost as frequently as the British go to pubs; but there the resemblance ends. The French café is a prized institution, privately owned and personally run. If it has bowed a little to the times, with television tucked away in a corner, a defective pin-ball machine for bar football, and occasionally if you are really unlucky, a juke-box, its proud place in French society remains intact.

A café differs from a British pub in three important aspects. Its opening and closing hours are entirely at the whim of the proprietor; families are uniformly welcome; and no one will think it the least strange if you spend as little money as possible and make your drinks last for hours.

Having said that, do not expect a French café to be particularly cheap. The mark-up on drinks, when compared to the equivalent in an off-licence, is considerable. To save money, sit at the bar, in French slang *le zinc.* (Canny folk who sit first at the bar then take their drinks back to the table always find when they come to pay, that they are still charged at the waiter service rate.) The cheapest drink is invariably *un café*, which is a small black coffee, sometimes called *un express* if it is made with an espresso machine behind the bar. *Un café crème* will produce more or less the same size cup, but with a little milk or cream; if you want a large, white coffee, ask for *un grand café au lait*, but be prepared for it to come very milky.

Tea is served without milk or lemon unless you specifically ask for it. Milk always seems in short supply in a French café, so expect a mildly hostile reaction to requests for a glass, even for children. However, all the standard fizzy and non-fizzy drinks are available, along with mineral water, though usually costing more than a glass of wine (*vin rouge, vin blanc*, rarely more choice than that). Real, rather than synthetic, orange juice is *un jus d'orange;* much more popular is *un citron pressé,* freshly squeezed lemon juice that usually arrives with water and sugar so that you can dilute it or sweeten it, if you choose. Both are expensive.

**Children and drinks**
The rules on serving alcoholic drinks to children under 14 are now stricter in France. A common drink for young teenage children who might be over 14 but probably are not, is *un panaché,* the equivalent of a shandy, though not always served with lemonade. For beer proper, the most common and therefore usually the cheapest, is *une pression,* literally a glass of pressurised keg beer. It may come in a bigger glass than you anticipated, unless you ask for *un demi,* slightly less than half a pint. Bottled beer is, however, made predominantly in northern France and a great many varieties may be on offer. Be warned that their alcoholic content in some cases is a great deal higher than in the UK, so a prudent driver should have one beer at the most. Foreign (i.e. non-French) beers may be even stronger and much more expensive.

*The food may be different too*

So is whisky, considered a prestigious drink ordered only by someone who can plainly afford it (and we can't, at French prices). Equally pricey as *le scotch* is *le gin-tonic* which may also, incidentally, prove to be a very strong double. It is prudent to order an extra tonic, which is *avec Schweppes* even if the tonic manufacturer proves not to be you know who.

You will have deduced from this that the French drink something else, and it certainly is not sherry, practically unknown and requested only by eccentric foreigners. What a French bar offers in abundance are apéritifs, of which Dubonnet is the most famous, some very sweet, some rather dry, some made with aniseed or liquorice, such as the equally prominent Pernod or Ricard. These particular drinks always arrive together with a jug of water, which when added makes the drink look more like diluted antiseptic. They are, however, extremely agreeable, and have the advantage that they can be stretched almost to infinity simply by adding water at intervals.

Eating in French cafés is never entirely successful. The concept of proper bar food has yet to reach France, and a sandwich bears no resemblance to those available in the UK. It consists of a huge chunk of French bread, split lengthways, sometimes buttered but just as often not, with a wedge of cheese or pâté or ham in the middle. Its only advantage is that horrible children can be silenced by challenging them to open their mouth wide enough to bite through it in one go – an inevitable, and painful, failure. The irony is that it fits the description of the instant meal created by John Montagu, the fourth Earl of Sandwich, back in 1762 when he refused to leave a gaming table in order to eat.

But not even Lord Sandwich thought of the *croque-monsieur*, literally man-toast, which shows how hopeless literal translations can be. This is a speciality of many cafés, a delicious toasted sandwich with a mixture of cheese and ham. If the ham is offered liberally, it may be called a *croque-madame*, the more luxurious version.

Do not ask for the bill until you are ready to leave, as nothing is more calculated to irritate the French than a foreigner who expects the bill to be added up more than once. Never try to pay when you order, or when your drink arrives.

## Restaurants

The bridge between cafés and restaurants is *la brasserie,* which once meant only a brewery, so it can be presumed that alcohol, rather than food, was once its priority. But while *la brasserie* will serve you a single dish for most of the day, a restaurant expects you to eat (or at any rate, to pay for) a complete meal, at the prescribed hours for lunch or dinner.

By law, every French restaurant has to display its menus outside, complete with prices, so that you can see the cost of what you fancy. Restaurants must also offer at least one fixed price menu, in which service and taxes are included, allowing customers to be certain, drinks apart, of what they will be asked to pay.

French restaurants differ from British in two important respects. First, most of them have only one sitting. Secondly, a much broader stratum of French society eats out on a regular basis. The French put a higher priority on eating out, helped, it must be said, by the fact that the cost of a restaurant meal in real terms represents a much smaller part of their disposable income. In consequence there are many more, family-run, widely patronised restaurants offering a high standard of cooking at reasonable prices.

Some gaffes (and after all, the French invented the word) to avoid:

Do not call the waiter 'garçon', he may also be the owner;

Do not expect to get through your meal like an express train – eating in France or Belgium is an important matter, not to be rushed;

Do not expect meat to be cooked the same way as in Britain – if you want, for example, a 'medium' steak, ask for *bien cuit,* literally 'well done'; *à point* is the British equivalent of 'rare'; *bleu* means that it has scarcely touched the pan;

Do not order the *menu touristique,* which often consists of cheap dishes for ignorant tourists; or the *menu gastronomique,* unless you have a huge appetite and a huge budget;

Do not expect a menu that includes wine *(boisson compris)* to mean that you will get the best bottle of wine in the house;

Do not expect coffee to be included;

Do not go to a restaurant for lunch on Sundays without booking, as this is the day most French families eat out;

Do not go to a restaurant for Sunday dinner unless it cannot be avoided; many are closed, and at those that are not, it may well be the chef's night off.

## Hotels and hostelries

There are several sound guides offering advice on where to stay, whose recommendations, while not infallible, result in few disappointments:

*Guide des Relais Routiers:* believed to have been financed, back in 1934, by some Parisian businessmen who wanted to be sure that they and their mistresses could have an agreeable weekend. At any rate, it is still going strong, and an invaluable guide for overnight stops.

*Michelin (Rouge):* surely the most successful sponsored product in motoring history. Its huge list of recommended hotels is updated annually, and ruthlessly weeded out.

*Logis et Auberges de France:* offers a list of several thousand, family-run hotels, cheap and comfortable.

*RAC Continental Motoring Guide:* includes a directory of RAC Appointed hotels and is updated annually.

Advance booking is advisable from mid-June to mid-September. By all means book by telephone, if necessary in pidgin French (though more and more hotels have at least one member of the family or staff who speaks some English), and confirm in writing in English. Do not be surprised if even when you make a firm booking and enclose an International Reply Coupon, no letter of confirmation arrives. Most French hotel owners reckon that if you can be bothered to write, then you will be bothered to turn up, and your booking is safe enough.

But only until 6 pm. Around that hour, the pragmatic nature of the French proprietor begins to assert itself. He may have another couple with a well-filled wallet and a flash-looking car positively panting to take over your room. If you cannot avoid arriving late, it is a good idea to remind the hotelier of your intentions by telephone.

Even if you have booked months in advance, it is well after 6 pm and you know, and the proprietor knows you know, that it is the only decent place for miles, still go through the ritual of asking to see your room. Every hotel has one or two rooms which are difficult to let, whether because they are too big and too expensive, or on the side of the hotel where the juggernauts change gear from dusk to dawn, or because they are linen cupboards converted to provide a single room for the impoverished travelling salesman. If you do not ask to see your room before committing yourself to stay, you run the risk that this is the kind of place where you will spend the night.

*A meal outside tastes all the better*

## Charges

Hotels charge the same amount for rooms more or less irrespective of the number of people using them, which is fine for families or very close friends. Most beds come with the famous French bolster *(lè traversin)* instead of proper pillows. If a search of the wardrobe proves fruitless, go back down to the proprietor and ask for a pillow *(un oreiller)* for each occupant of the room. He will probably manage to convey the impression that the British are pathetic weaklings, but any humiliation is better than wrestling with a bolster all night.

Blankets, extra, visitors for the use of, are a rather better bet, but except in first-class hotels, expect to supply your own soap. Once again the proprietor, under duress, may come up with a miniscule bar *(une savonette),* which he will probably add to your bill. However he will only begin to resemble a French version of Basil Fawlty if you complain about the level of lighting in your room, and ask for the bulbs to be changed. A speciality of small French hotels is to have several bulbs which have not worked for years or are of so low a wattage that you still need a torch to read by. The truly cynical and experienced traveller keeps in his car a box of assorted light bulbs, bayonet and screw, large and small fittings, to outwit the hotelier who is trying to keep his overheads down to the bare minimum.

## Plumbing

Rooms with a private bathroom complete with a toilet are still comparatively rare in smaller French hotels. This is because while running extra pipes and increasing the size of the boiler is a simple plumbing exercise, private toilets require major changes to the sanitation, which in most instances is certainly best left untouched – as it has probably been for years.

Although the standard of hygiene is as high in France and Belgium as it is in the UK, Continental travellers seem more willing to traipse down the passageway in the middle of the night to use the loo. They also seem prepared to put up with eccentric showers that would defy a professor of mathematics to find the precise spot on their controls that guarantees a continuous stream of water at the right temperature. But you can be sure that no matter how indifferent the rest of their bathroom facilities, every one will contain a bidet. It looks like a knee-high toilet but is designed for intimate bathing and attempts to use it for anything else can have disastrous, and embarrassing, results.

## Breakfast

After bed, breakfast. Given the French incapacity to make proper tea, then coffee, or hot chocolate, is a much better bet. It comes with croissants (delicious crescent-shaped rolls) a selection of French bread, butter and preserves. However, do not expect marmalade, it is almost unknown in France; if you cannot do without it, take a small pot of your own. Breakfast is almost always charged separately from the room, and is expensive for what it is when compared with dinner the previous night. Unless you are staying out in the wilds, getting dressed and going to the café round the corner will result in a much better breakfast at half the price.

## Shops

When Napoleon was overheard to make a scathing remark about a 'nation of shopkeepers' while standing on the cliffs near Boulogne, everyone failed to notice that he had his back to the Channel. It was the French he was referring to. Theory? But of course, though a plausible one, for if ever there were a nation of shopkeepers, it must be not the English, but the French.

### Food first

In sharp contrast to the United Kingdom, small shops are believed to be on the increase in France, not in decline. In a country where quality and service are much appreciated, the small man survives, in spite of his higher prices. But at considerable personal cost.

Take for example, *la boulangerie,* the baker's shop. An ancient French law prac-

*The local bakery; wherever you are you'll find one near you*

tically forbids them to go out of existence, and by popular demand they have to be open from first thing in the morning until last thing at night. Because of the French fanatical insistence on fresh bread, the baker himself may well be up at 3.30 am, including Sundays, and apart from an afternoon siesta, still baking away at 6 or 7 pm. He cannot even put up his prices, because they, too, are fixed by law.

If you are buying bread, for example for use later on a roadside picnic, simply point to what you want. A typical long French loaf is called *une baguette,* the huge round rustic-looking loaf is usually known as *un pain de campagne.* Most bakers also sell *croissants,* and not just at breakfast, *brioches,* which are sweet buns, and *les pains au chocolat,* rich bread with chocolate inside – very popular with children.

Cake in France is a gâteau, light and creamy. *La pâtisserie,* which may be next door or even part of the baker's empire, produces superb gâteaux, fresh fruit tarts, delicious éclairs, and other tempting sweetmeats. They are more a main meal course than a tea-time delicacy and *le pâtissier* likes nothing better than to make up an advance order in a presentation box. Sunday morning is his big day, as gâteaux are frequently eaten at Sunday lunch, along with another of his products, homemade ice cream. Steel yourself for a huge bill.

*L'alimentation:* baffling. Each one seems to sell something different, and never exactly what you went in for. Nearly all have crisps, biscuits and tinned foods – though these are far less popular in France or Belgium than in the UK. Others offer dairy products, fruit and vegetables.

*L'épicerie:* a grocer's with a very wide brief, as, if his shop is large enough, part of it will look like a dairy, another section like a greengrocer's, a third, like an up-market off-licence.

*La boucherie:* meat in a Continental butcher's shop is sometimes better value for money than its British equivalent, because the butcher cuts up the meat in a different way. Put simply, he does not provide 'joints', but 'cuts', which are sliced

along the muscles rather than across them. Most meat is sold free of bones and excess fat, and what is weighed is often entirely edible.

Most butchers sell beef, lamb, mutton, veal, sometimes game and poultry, but rarely pork, unless he is a *boucherie-charcuterie* (for *charcuterie*, see below). If you want steak, do not ask for *le bifteck*, because this implies that you are not fussy about quality. Try to use one of the correct terms for particular cuts, *filet, contre-filet, entrecôte, rumsteck, faux-filet.* If you are making hamburgers, ask for *bifteck haché,* which is fat-free minced beef. Lamb chops are *côtes* (or côtelettes) *d'agneau* and a leg of lamb is a *gigot.*

Poultry *(volailles)* is sold fresh, be it free-range or battery reared. A free-range chicken, *poulet fermier,* costs nearly twice as much but may be well worth the extra. Be warned, however, that birds are usually sold complete with head and feet unless you ask for them to be removed.

A potential gaffe: *La boucherie chevaline* sells horsemeat, and has a clearly identifiable large red or gold representation of a horse's head above the shop door. Although the meat tastes and costs much the same as beef, the animal-loving British firmly draw the line at eating it.

*La charcuterie:* the word comes from the description, *chair cuite,* or cooked meat, the meat being predominantly pork. *Chair* or flesh still exists as a kind of raw sausage meat. *La charcuterie* today is more of a delicatessen, offering an enormous range of succulent pâtés and pies, pizzas, quiche and salads, in fact all kinds of ready prepared dishes (sometimes in a separate shop, *le traîteur),* in which, not unreasonably, you pay for the labour involved. Most items in *la charcuterie* are sold by the slice *(une tranche).*

*La poissonnerie:* a fishmonger's is more common as a market stall then as a traditional shop, and it remains a trade secret exactly how they succeed in providing fresh fish however far you are from the sea (probably an energetic younger son who likes driving lorries, and is an insomniac). Many varieties of seafood are on offer, though you may want to sample them first at a local restaurant as *un plateau de fruits de mer* before plunging in to purchase. Of the usual fish sold in the United Kingdom, sole and turbot are the same words, differently pronounced of course; whiting is *merlan;* and cod, *cabillaud.* The fishmonger will clean *(vider)* and fillet *(découper en filets)* the fish if you want him too.

**Opening times** From Tuesday to Saturday inclusive, many food shops open as early as 7.30 in the morning, close surprisingly promptly at noon and reopen around 3 pm, perhaps later in hotter parts of France. They stay open until at least 7 pm and sometimes 8 pm. On Sundays, they usually open a little later in the morning and are certainly shut by midday. On Mondays, to compensate for a gruelling week, they may well be closed all morning and sometimes all day.

### Les Grands Magasins

The world's first department store was the Marble Dry Goods Palace, opened in New York in 1848 by Alexander Turney Stewart. At the time it was built it was also certainly the largest shop in the world, as it extended over the length of a block in the exclusive Broadway district. But the French were the first to appreciate the true potential of the department store, *les grands magasins,* with the opening of the Bon Marché on the left bank of the Seine in the autumn of 1852. It was a stupendous success, and led to other Parisian businessmen getting together to create Galeries Lafayette and Au Printemps, both on the Boulevard Haussmann. From these shops has grown up a French tradition of department stores in every town, which, if comparatively modest in size, do try to provide a huge range of goods at reasonable prices.

Two familiar shop names throughout France are Monoprix and Prisunic, both of which are now subsidiaries of Galeries Lafayette and Au Printemps, a case of if you can't beat them, join them. They are laid out like Woolworth or Marks and Spencer in this country so shopping there presents no difficulty, although the days when everything they sold was exactly the same price, hence their names, have sadly gone long ago. They take credit cards and in tourist areas they often accept travellers cheques or even sterling (ask at the cash desk when you go in). In some stores, if you know you are certain to buy a lot, request *un carnet d'achats,* so that you need pay only once, when you leave.

### Along the High Street

*Le tabac:* strictly speaking *le bureau de tabac,* because of its official status as the only outlet for stamps (apart from the post office) and cigarettes (apart from hotels and smart restaurants). However, don't expect the tobacconist to be an expert on the sea rate for a parcel from Boulogne to Bali. If you want cigarettes, home-produced French brands are the cheapest and the strongest; ask for *un paquet,* a packet, as they are all sold in 20s.

*La droguerie:* despite its name it does not sell drugs. It does however have a few items associated with a chemist's shop in the UK: soap, hair-pins, scissors, combs, shampoo. Its principal wares are for the household, such as brushes, detergents, polish, light bulbs, rubbish bags, corkscrews and tin openers, also cutlery, cooking utensils, crockery.

*La quincaillerie:* a kind of ironmonger's, catering for most do-it-yourself enthusiasts and selling everything metallic including

| Food to take abroad with you | |
|---|---|
| **Sweets** | heat-resistant (so avoid most chocolate) varieties because the French home-made equivalent is hugely expensive. |
| **Biscuits** | if there are particular varieties of British biscuit that you, or the children, especially like |
| **Breakfast cereals** | rarely eaten on the Continent, except in international hotels; and when available, very expensive |
| **Marmalade** | *la confiture d'oranges* is occasionally available, at a price, but the chunky kind, almost never |
| **Sauces and spreads** | Tomato ketchup apart, the French do not use bottled sauces on their food, and regard those who do with consternation. If you are a Worcester Sauce or H.P. addict, take it with you. Bisto and Marmite are of course spreads not sauces, but are as unobtainable. |
| **Baked beans** | in French *haricots à la sauce tomate*; but the sauce that accompanies them would be rejected by most British children. |
| **Coffee** | Instant coffee, *café soluble*, would never be served in any self-respecting French or Belgian household, and while you can buy it, the price seems almost designed to deter you from doing so. |
| **Tea** | Much more expensive than in Britain. Strictly speaking, you are supposed to import only 100 grams (just under ¼lb per person), but this quota applies to baby too. |

household goods. This is where to go for tools and screws.

*La pharmacie:* French law requires the pharmacist to own and operate his own shop, to be a qualified dispensing chemist and to have considerable training in general medical matters. Many drugs available only on prescription in the United Kingdom can be purchased over the counter on the Continent. It pays therefore to be careful what you buy and to follow the instructions carefully. Apart from international brands such as Alka-Seltzer, Kleenex, Tampax, and so on, the pharmacist will also stock the favourite French remedy for 'holiday tummy'. This is called *l'élixir parégorique,* and contains opium flavoured with aniseed; it tastes a bit like Pernod or Ricard.

*La blanchisserie:* a laundry; launderettes (called *la blanchisserie automatique*) are comparatively rare. Dry cleaning takes place at *le pressing,* where you may find a 'service wash' . . . at a price.

*La cordonnerie:* the shoemenders will often patch up your shoes while you wait, but proper repairs usually take a few days. Look out for *un talon minute,* a heel bar, in big department stores.

If you want a newspaper, look for a sign that says *journaux* or for *une maison de la presse.* British newspapers are available in all the Channel ports served by Dover.
**Opening hours** Apart from food shops, most shops open around 9.30 but otherwise keep similar hours, except Sunday, when they are invariably closed. Department stores stay open throughout the day.

**Hypermarkets**
Hypermarkets have the longest opening hours of all. Most of them are open from 9 am until 10 pm, without interruption, from Monday to Saturday. They are, however, usually closed on Sundays. Do not be misled by the fact that you can see people coming in and out of their cafeteria: because Sunday is such a big eating-out occasion in France, hypermarkets reckon that it is worth opening their cafeteria even when the rest of the shop is firmly shut.

There are now over 350 hypermarkets in France worthy of the name. But there lies a problem. Because a hypermarket is, literally, a hype, an enlarged or exaggerated supermarket, the temptation placed in front of supermarkets to move up a category is hard to resist. Some hypermarkets creeping into prominence are really only average-sized supermarkets. However, in the area close to the northern Channel ports, the chains run by Continent and Auchan do offer the huge range of products that the name hypermarket leads the shopper to expect.

Some hypermarkets take credit cards, or even sterling, although the rate of exchange is not particularly favourable. Suggested purchases which are either unobtainable in the UK or would cost a great deal more if bought at home are listed on pages 149–151.

| British and Continental clothing sizes | | | | | | |
|---|---|---|---|---|---|---|
| **Ladies' sizes** (bust) | | | | | | |
| British | 8/30 | 10/32 | 12/34 | 14/36 | 16/38 | 18/40 |
| Continental | 38/34N | 40/36N | 42/38N | 44/40N | 46/42N | 48/44N |
| **Men's sizes** (chest) | | | | | | |
| British | 34 | 36 | 38 | 40 | 42 | 44 | 46 |
| Continental | 44 | 46 | 48 | 50 | 52 | 54 | 56 |
| (collar) | | | | | | |
| British | 14 | 14½ | 15 | 15½ | 16 | 16½ | 17 |
| Continental | 36 | 37 | 38 | 39 | 40 | 41 | 42 |
| **Shoe sizes** | | | | | | |
| British | 3 | 4 | 5 | 6 | 7 | 8 | 9 | 10 | 11 | 12 |
| Continental | 36 | 37 | 38 | 40 | 41 | 42 | 43 | 44 | 45 | 46 |

# Sur le Continent

## Where to go and what to do in and around the five Channel ports

*The Cathedral dome and the narrow streets of Old Boulogne*

## Boulogne

Once a popular place from which to invade Britain – Julius Caesar, Napoleon and Hitler all attempted it with variable degrees of success – Boulogne now plays host to the British themselves in ever-increasing numbers. For shopping, it offers almost instant access to the main streets opposite the harbour; for sight-seeing, charming cobbled streets high on the hill, enclosed by ancient city walls.

Boulogne first appears on the map in Roman times, when it was a prominent harbour, Gessoriacum, later called Bononia. It may have been from here that Julius Caius Caesar set out in 55 BC at the second attempt to conquer the Ancient Britons, taking his legions across the Channel in 800 boats; in those days, no mean logistical exercise.

By 636 Boulogne was secure and stable enough to build a Cathedral, Notre Dame: on the site of the original Roman temple. A popular legend was that a statue of the Virgin Mary, standing upright in an open boat, had been pushed ashore by Angels to consecrate the Cathedral. Each August the event is commemorated by a procession through the town, carrying the statue of the Madonna, although the ravages of time make the present statue, at a conservative estimate, at least the fifth to fulfill the role.

The original Madonna is supposed to have survived an attack by the Norsemen in 882 when Boulogne was all but razed to the ground and did not reappear as a taxation collecting point – always a sure sign of a town's existence – for 30 years. Its prosperity was not assured until 1477 when King Louis XI pronounced the statue to be the true statue of the Madonna and that the town was under the care of Notre Dame, the Vatican gave money to restore the Cathedral, and pilgrims flocked to Boulogne, creating its first tourist industry.

The Cathedral was thereafter regarded as a particularly holy place, so much so that 14 French and five English Kings have prayed before its altar. In 1308, Edward II married Isabella, daughter of the French King Philip IV, in the Cathedral crypt. That Edward agreed to leave English soil for the marriage, emphasizes how the English were then little more than the vassals of the French. It proved, however, to be less than a success from the French point of view because the son of Edward and Isabella, Edward III, became the principal claimant to the French throne and in pursuing his birthright began a war between England and France that lasted for One Hundred Years, hence its name. In 1420, following the Treaty of Troyes, Boulogne was recognised as an English fiefdom – but only for 15 years.

Another English king, Henry VIII, laid seige to Boulogne and took it in 1544. Boulogne remained British for six years, acquiring from Henry's Welsh foot soldiers a culinary skill (still surviving) in the making of Welsh rarebit, but little else. Boulogne was sold back to Henri II of France for 200,000 gold ducats, an immense sum in those days, a payment the French king subsequently regretted when he discovered that the English army had taken with them almost everything that could be moved. Whether or not the good citizens of Boulogne were grateful to their king for recovering the town for France is not recorded, but they did insert a likeness of him in the town's ramparts.

The ramparts themselves were built by the Count of Boulogne in the 13th century. At that time the answer to the ever-increasing potency of cannon and gunpowder was thought to be to increase the size and number of fortifications. As a consequence, the ramparts of Boulogne have massive walls so thick that gardens have been cultivated on top of them, obscuring their original purpose. Adjoining the ramparts is the castle which was built by Philippe Hurepel between 1231 and 1235, using, much to later archaeologists' dismay, a great deal of material from the original Roman fortifications on the same site.

For the statistically minded, the ramparts contain 17 towers and four fortified gateways, one of which, the Porte des Degrés, was closed from the start of Henry VIII's siege in 1544 until 1895, and even now is open only for pedestrians. From the towers to the south it is possible to see the white cliffs of Dover on a clear day, just as Pilâtre de Rozier may well have done on the morning of June 15, 1785, when he attempted to cross the Channel by hot-air balloon. De Rozier,

*The massive 13th-century ramparts*

together with the Marquis d'Arlande, had been one of the first humans to fly in the Montgolfier hot-air balloon over Paris in November, 1783. But already, on January 7 1785, the feat of crossing the Channel had been achieved – from Dover to France – by Colonel Jean-Pierre Blanchard and an American, Dr John Jeffries, using a hydrogen balloon. Rozier was nevertheless determined to become the first man to cross in the other direction and was launched with a companion, Romain, from the Gayette Tower. For a few minutes all went well, Rozier reached 1800 feet, but suddenly his balloon fell apart and he crashed at Wimille, just outside Boulogne, the first fatal casualty in the history of ballooning. You can see a memorial column to Blanchard and Jeffries in a remote spot in the forest of Guînes, northwest of Boulogne; Rozier, who was buried in the cemetery at Wimille, has to make do with a modest plaque in the Gayette Tower.

The ramparts completely enclose the Haut Ville, as the old town on the hill is called, and a walk right round, at most a leisurely half hour, gives you a marvellous view of Boulogne old and new. Dominating the Old Town is the Cathedral of Notre Dame, built between 1827 and 1866. The Italian dome, decorated by the Papal craftsmen, was described by the early Victorian traveller Augustus Hare as "pretentious and ill-proportioned" but then he was, later on, to make equally scathing comments about the Pantheon. What is beyond dispute is the attractiveness of the Norman crypt, honeycombed with tiny passages, which afforded its

*Boulogne's harbour today*

bishops both cool seclusion and a means of protection from unwelcome visitors. The Cathedral itself has two exceptional pieces whose common feature is their creation out of a single section of raw material, a statue of St Joseph, made from an enormous block of Carrara marble; and a statue of Notre Dame, carved out of a 1,000-year-old cedar tree.

The Cathedral's altar must not be missed. A present, in 1866, from an Italian prince, it arrived in Boulogne in nine sections on a series of ornate wagons pulled by 36 magnificent white stallions. It was created in the Papal workshops by three men regarded as masters of their craft – the design came from the architect Carnavali, it was sculpted by the stone mason Leonardi, and the mosaics were added by Rinaldi. So perfect are the sections of marble, so well integrated are the precious stones, nearly 150 different varieties, that the joins are almost invisible. Biblical figures have been created in exquisite detail, notably the Apostles and the Virgin Mary.

The counts of Boulogne had their palace in the centre of the

Haut Ville; all that remains is the 13th century Belfry. Next to it is the elegant 18th century town hall, the Hôtel de Ville. The present municipal library, opposite the town hall, was originally a lodging house (for the first tourist-pilgrims), then a hospital, a convent and, during the French Revolution, a prison. Now restored, both the building and its delightful cloistered garden are open to the public. Nearby are the two atmospheric old town squares, Place Godefroy de Bouillon, named after a local knight who led the first Crusade to Jerusalem; and the self-evident Place de la Résistance.

### Napoleon in Boulogne

Napoleon Bonaparte made his headquarters in the Old Town at the Hôtel Desandrouin, renamed the Imperial Palace, while he was planning the invasion of England. The project took the best part of three years, during which time Napoleon enlarged Boulogne harbour to accommodate the 2,000 barges he needed to transport his Grand Army across the Channel. His troops slept under canvas on the nearby hillsides, forbidden to go into Boulogne at the insistence of the town council, although what might discreetly be termed certain amusements were taken each evening to the tent city itself.

Napoleon's advance planning even included a victory column, the Colonne de la Grande Armée (still to be seen 5 kilometres north of the town) with a statue of himself in bronze, and medals for his troops enscribed "Descente en Angleterre, frappé à Londres". Inconveniently, however, Admiral Nelson destroyed all French hope of dominating the seas by his victory at Trafalgar, and in 1805 when the Austrians put a new army into the field, Napoleon marched off to meet them. Afterwards, people remembered that the statue had been erected with Napoleon standing with his back to the Channel; an omen, they said.

You can see what English cartoonists thought of the failure of the invasion plans in a collection of prints in Boulogne's museum in the Grande Rue. The collection of antiquities is remarkable for a provincial town, as it includes Greek, Roman and Egyptian treasures, some of the Egyptian acquired by Napoleon's troops on their expedition to Egypt. Also on display is Napoleon's hat, although suffice it to say, if all those in French museums were ever gathered together, it would be concluded that Napoleon wore, or at any rate owned, an astonishing number of hats of sharply different sizes. Another museum in the Grande Rue is the house of General San Martin who led the army that liberated Argentina, Chile and Peru from Spanish domination. He retired to

*Master cheesemaker Philippe Olivier*

Boulogne and his statue stands near the casino by the beach which is called after him.

This wide sandy beach has been a popular spot for sea bathing since the Revolutionary relaxation of the church law that forbade mixed bathing. In the 19th century, sea bathing became so popular it was possible to hire bathing huts, parasols and other beach paraphernalia. Edouard Manet, the great French painter, recorded a delightful beach scene at Boulogne-sur-Mer, as it had now become, when donkey rides were already much in evidence. Charles Dickens was another famous English visitor to Boulogne. He stayed in the nearby village of Condotte, where he wrote much of *Hard Times* and *Bleak House;* and, it must be said, devoted some time to an actress called Ellen Ternan.

The British had 'invaded' Boulogne again in the 19th century. 'One of the chief British colonies abroad. The town is enriched by English

money; warmed, lighted and stoked by English coal; English signs and advertisements decorate every other shop door, inn, tavern and lodging house; almost every third person you meet is either a countryman or speaking our language.'

That was Boulogne in 1842, according to Murray's Handbook, when an unofficial local census showed that of 30,000 inhabitants, 4,800 were British. As, like most censuses, it relied for its accuracy on people volunteering information, it is likely that the actual number of British subjects was considerably higher. Many of those who did not want it put abroad that that was indeed where they were, had been pursued to Dover, or literally to the three-mile limit, by the most determined bailiffs or officers of the court, after being found guilty of a crime under British law. The most common was debt, and many Britons now found the Boulogne shopkeepers gullible prey, until they in their turn called in the law and the debtors found themselves behind French bars instead. Indeed, so numerous were the British prisoners in Boulogne jail in the 19th century, that it was known as 'L'Hôtel d'Angleterre'.

## World War II

Boulogne is proud of the fact that French troops held Boulogne against Germany's second Panzer Division, a testament both to their courage and to the improvements in the fortifications made as far back as the 17th century by Louis XIV's military genius, Vauban. It was only on May 26, 1940, that Boulogne fell to the Germans. Soon Hitler was filmed walking on Cap Gris Nez and peering across the Channel towards England. Soon Boulogne's harbour was full of barges, waiting for the seas and the skies to be cleared by the Luftwaffe; which was not to be.

That the Old Town survived at all is little short of a miracle, for during World War II the Royal Air Force flew more than 400 sorties against Boulogne when bombing was, at best, a hit and miss affair. The rest of the town was flattened and not rebuilt to advantage, although the Place Dalton is transformed on market days, Wednesdays and Saturdays. Saturday is the busier morning of the two, from as early as 7am until lunchtime, with stalls and vans mainly owned by the local farmers. The presentation of the food they sell is fascinating and the range of vegetables prodigious. One stall sells nothing but nuts and dried fruit; another fresh salads; a third everything from pumpkins to garlic. If only out of

curiosity, count the queues at the horsemeat van, a favourite of the French; but steel your heart at the boxes of live rabbits, nibbling away noisily, still blissfully unaware that they are shortly destined to become someone's dinner.

The market also has a farm cheese stall with some powerfully smelling goat cheese, but for cheese there is really nothing to beat Philippe Olivier's shop in the rue Thiers. Olivier was the youngest man ever to become a Master Cheesemaker of France, and he sells nearly 200 different varieties made by the traditional methods in farms throughout France. Beneath the shop are five cellars where the cheeses are matured; these are sometimes open to visitors although Olivier is aware that becoming a tourist attraction is not necessarily good for business.

But Boulogne is first and foremost a fishing port, the largest in France and for that matter in the Common Market, with 100,000 tons of fish landed every year. Virtually every morning along the quai Gambetta at the end of the rue Faidherbe, right beside the bridge to the ferries, the fish market can be found selling produce straight from the boats. Mussels, oysters and all kinds of sea food are on offer, together with fish patés and terrines, stuffed mussels and dressed crab. Seafood restaurants therefore abound in Boulogne, from the luxurious La Matelote, named after a fish stew, to the stand-up fish and chippery. For whether you like it or not, chips are a permanent feature of all but the most discriminating cuisine in Boulogne and on peak days in summer the central area around the port is indistinguishable from a dozen British resorts, apart from the absence of opening and closing hours.

*Boulogne – premier fishing port of France*

## Shopping

In Boulogne, shoppers find it easy to get their bearings. When you come across the bridge over the harbour after leaving the ferry or hovercraft, all the principal shopping streets are within easy walk. Immediately in front of you is the rue Faidherbe, which will have traffic descending it from the Old Town; about 150 yards up it is rue Victor Hugo to the right; or about 250 yards up rue Faidherbe is rue Thiers, also to the right. Both rue Thiers and rue Victor Hugo lead into Grande Rue, another one-way street, this time with the traffic going up the hill. You need look no further for most purchases.

### Rue Faidherbe
*Griff* fashionable clothes, for both sexes
*Aux Bonnes Choses* wines and cheeses
*Florence* leather goods
*La Cave* electrical goods
*Desoomers* charcuterie
*Brûlerie Faidherbe* up-market groceries
*Laines Berger du Nord* wools and sweaters
*Prébaby* everything for young children
*L'Amirauté* boulangerie
*Monteil* milliner (if only to watch the French ladies trying on hats)

### Rue Thiers
*Philippe Olivier* cheeses, cheeses, cheeses (see p. 67)
*Descamps* Linen
*Nouvelles Galeries* the largest department store in Boulogne
*Au Cornet d'Amour* chocolates and sweetmeats
*Lafarge* leather goods
*Marose* perfume
*Natalys* everything for young children

### Rue Victor Hugo
*Artflor* plant and flowers
*Cheminée Selections* everything for fireplaces
*La Pendulerie* clocks
*Chouchouze* children's shoes

### Grande Rue
*Lugand Pâtisserie* tea and pâtisseries served in the shop or to take away
*Prisunic* strictly speaking in rue de la Lampe which is the port end of Grande Rue
*L'Aquarium* seashells, butterflies, fish
*Claude Debuiche* charcuterie
*Jouéclub* toys
*Derrien* charcuterie
*Parfumerie Gilliocq* perfumes and toiletries
*Luc et Lucie* for children's clothes
*Le Chais* cross Grande Rue from rue Victor Hugo, into rue Nationale; a good walk, then right into rue des Deux Points; complicated, but Le Chais is a wine shop well worth the effort.

### Markets
Place Dalton, Wednesday and Saturday mornings, for food; Boulevard de Clocheville, Wednesday and Saturday, for clothes.

### Hypermarket
'Auchan', not in Boulogne, but at La Capelle, four miles away in the St Omer direction, just off the N42. Enormous car park, and a bus service from the centre of Boulogne. Best sections – charcuterie, cheese, gardening implements, electrical goods. Sterling accepted, though at an unfavourable rate of exchange. Open 9am–10pm Tues–Sat, 2pm–10pm Mon, closed Sun.

### Parking
Meters everywhere, and also

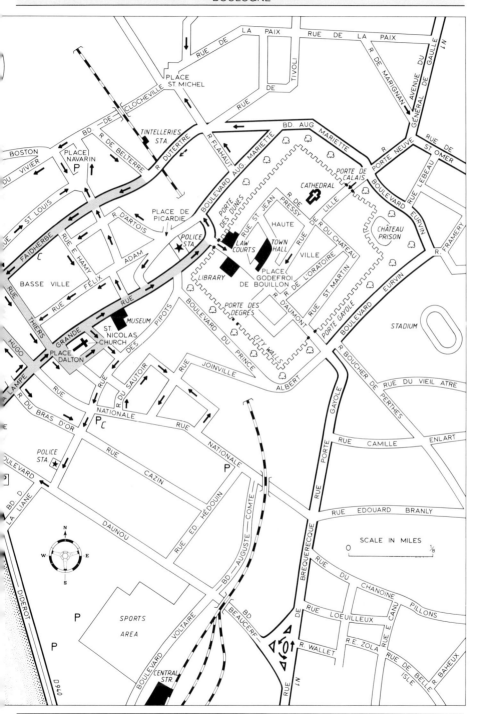

French traffic wardens; tourists are towed away as readily as locals, and it costs a small fortune and takes for ever to recover the car – so be warned. Down on the quai is a much better bet, and still not far to walk. Alternatively, try the Commercial Centre de la Liane off Boulevard Diderot, intended for those using the Champion Supermarket, but you do not have to.

### Changing money

Banks usually open 9am–noon, 2pm–5pm Monday to Friday. All those with branches in the Place Dalton, rue Faidherbe and rue Thiers have a change counter. Some British banks have branches, but you cannot obtain sterling direct or use your UK domestic cheque card to obtain money because of local regulations.

At weekends, use the Scalbert Dupont bureau de change at the ferry port (above the tourist office) or the hoverport. The ferry branch is normally open 9am–7pm and at the hoverport 9am–8pm in the summer season. Out of season, it is open only around the flight arrival and departure times.

### Tourist Offices

Pont Marguet Tel (21) 31 68 38. Closed Sun and Mon except high season.
Quai Chanzy, near ferry terminal, same telephone no., open July–September. For guided tours Tel (21) 92 11 52.

### Opening times

Notre Dame Cathedral: crypt 9am–noon, 2pm–6pm. Closed Mon pm, Tues am.
The Belfry (by Town Hall): 8am–noon, 2pm–6pm. Closed Sat pm, all Sun.
Municipal Library: 9.30am–noon, 2pm–6pm. Closed Sun and Mon.
Musée des Beaux Arts, 34 Grande Rue: 9.30am–noon, 2pm–6.30pm Wed–Sun.
House of San Martin: 10am–noon, 2pm–6pm Mon–Fri except fête days.
Colonne de la Grande Armée: 9am–noon, and 1.30pm–6pm, shorter hours October–May, closed most Tues and Wed.

### Accommodation

#### Hotels

*Metropole**** 51 rue Thiers, Tel (21) 31 54 30. Closed mid December – early January. Bed and Continental breakfast only. Beware rooms near lift. Friendly, but noisy.
*Faidherbe** 12 rue Faidherbe, Tel (21) 31 60 93. Bed and Continental breakfast only. Recently refurbished, but still a bit noisy.
*Lorraine** 7 Place de Lorraine, Tel (21) 31 34 78. Bed and Continental breakfast only. Closed mid December – mid January.
*Londres** 22 Place de France, Tel (21) 31 35 63. Bed and Continental breakfast only.
*La Plage* see restaurant section.

#### Restaurants

*La Matelote* 80 Boulevard Ste-Beuve, Tel (21) 30 17 97. Rates a Michelin star for outstanding cuisine. Predominantly fish. Closed Sun eve, Tues., second half June, mid December – early January. Expensive.
*La Liégoise* 10 rue A.-Monsigny, Tel (21) 31 61 15. Once famous, now less so – but more reasonably priced. Good local fish dishes. Closed Sun eve. Fri (which is surprising); mid January – 1 February.
*La Charlotte* 11 rue du Doyen (which is off Place Dalton), Tel (21) 30 13 08. Fish again. Closed Sun. Booking more or less essential. Ask for a downstairs table.
*La Plage* 124 Boulevard Sainte Beuve, Tel (21) 31 45 35. If you have too good a meal here even to drive to the ferry, there are inexpensive rooms available for the night; but it is as a restaurant that Michelin rate it. Very good value, as one might expect, as it is often packed with locals. The restaurant, but of course not the hotel, is closed on Mon., and, apart from the peak summer season, also on Sun eve.
*Hamiot* 1 rue Faidherbe, Tel (21) 31 44 20. You can discuss the price of cod with the local fishermen in the ground floor bar, where the atmosphere is frantic, and totally French. Waiters pass through with increasingly tempting dishes, so most tourists end upstairs in the restaurant. Outstanding value. Never admits to closing. Rooms available, but with the harbour on one wall and the main shopping street on the other, suitable only for an aunt with an ear trumpet.

There are 24 hotels and 36 restaurants registered with the Boulogne Office of Tourism, and probably a good many outside that. As a general rule, always ask for a hotel room overlooking one of the inside courtyards, but do not expect an uninterrupted night. Apart from some of those restaurants described above, if you want to avoid eating with a posse of fellow British, make for the Old Town and try your luck there. Although some way off the best, certainly the most bizarre name for a hotel/restaurant can be found in the Boulevard Danou: it is called simply: Au Sleeping.

# Calais

The closest Continental port to Britain and in many ways it has the closest ties. More people are said to speak English here than do in Paris. It is in reality two towns in one: Calais by the harbour and St Pierre to the south, each with its own shopping centre. The town hall lies in St Pierre and is heavily ornate, with a huge belfry; it looks old Flemish but is actually modern.

### Burghers of Calais

In pride of place in front of the town hall you will find the six burghers statue by Auguste Rodin. The six burghers were the brave citizens of Calais who in 1347 offered their lives to the English king, Edward III, if he would spare the town.

Edward had been held up at Calais in a siege lasting eight months, and was probably in no mood to spare anyone, but he was won round by his French Queen, Philippa of Hainault.

The economic interdependence of England and the cities of Flanders, because of the wool trade, made Calais a vital gateway to the Continent, and it remained English for more than 200 years.

Henry VIII held a summit meeting with the French king, François I, on June 7, 1520, near Calais, on what was evidently a glittering display of chivalry in the Field of the Cloth of Gold (see p. 90). The loss of Calais on January 7, 1558, to the Duke of Guise, after England had been drawn into the Spanish war with France, certainly hastened the death of England's unhappy queen, Mary. 'When I am dead and opened,' she is supposed to have lamented, 'you shall find 'Calais' lying in my heart.' England's dismay and incredulity at this defeat were best summed up by an inscription left behind on one of the gates to the town: 'When shall the Frenchman Calais win, when iron and lead like corks shall swim.'

The only permanent evidence of English rule is the 13th century church in the Place d'Armes which is built in English Perpendicular style, and where, in 1921, Charles de Gaulle married a Calais girl. But Calais' connection with de Gaulle did not amount to much when it came to rebuilding the shattered port after the Liberation, because Dunkerque and Boulogne, even more badly

*Rodin's statue of the Burghers of Calais stands in front of the Town Hall*

damaged, were given priority. Although Dunkerque was the historical symbol of a heroic British retreat, Calais had its moment in 1940 when a company of Green Jackets held up the German advance from a minute island in the harbour. Calais has its own little war museum near the town hall, on the site of the German Navy's wartime telephone exchange.

Beyond the harbour to the west is Calais beach, a magnificent stretch of sand as good as any on the coast, where the more energetic visitor can indulge in the unusual sport of sand yachting. If the wind blows a little stronger than the bather might like, the sea is in fact significantly warmer than on the English side of the Channel because of favourable currents. Still further west is Blériot-Plage, from where Louis Blériot set out to fly the Channel on July 25, 1909. He landed near Dover 37 minutes later: he'd have beaten the hovercraft.

The best place to see the whole of Calais is the lighthouse, provided that you feel fit enough: it stands 170ft above the port, with 271 steps to the lighting chamber. The lighthouse is open to visitors in July and August (and by request at other times). Make sure that there are no school parties on the way if you climb to the top: otherwise you could be stuck up there for hours.

The old vantage point was the 13th century Watch Tower in the Place d'Armes, one of the few ancient buildings to have survived in Calais. Nearby is the moated citadelle with its tranquil gardens which provide a welcome place of retreat from the noise and bustle of Calais' shopping streets.

**Famous visitors**

Calais may have become French again in the 16th century but the English have continued to pass through it to places further afield. Although it happened more than 200 years ago, the arrival of one of Calais' most illustrious English visitors can be measured to the minute. At 10.30 am on Thursday, October 23, 1783, Horatio Nelson stepped off a packet boat in Calais harbour after a crossing from Dover that had taken 3½ hours. We know the exact details because Nelson was an obsessive letter writer, and devoted several pages to a description of Calais and its sights that would not exactly have induced others to follow in his tracks.

Nelson was 25, a captain in the British Navy, and on leave in one of those intermittent periods when England was actually not at war with anyone. He stayed only half a day in Calais, breakfasting at the Grandsire's Inn, and touring the town in a post-chaise, which he found, in disagreeable contrast to those for hire on

the other side of the Channel, possessed no springs whatsoever. His tour of northern France was a leisurely one, for he had got no further than St Omer by Christmas, detained by a lady despite his almost non-existent French.

Nelson never came back to Calais, but his beloved Lady Hamilton, alas, ended her days there in abject poverty, dying on January 15, 1815. Despite Nelson's intentions, neither his country nor his last will and testament provided for his mistress and their illegitimate daughter, Horatia.

After Trafalgar, and the death of Nelson, Lady Hamilton fell into debt and was twice imprisoned before sailing for France in July, 1814. Known locally as plain Emma Lyons, a native of Lancashire, she settled in a farmhouse in what was then the small village of St Pierre (now Calais Sud), but moved into Calais for the winter, where she fell ill and died, through a combination of jaundice and heavy drinking. Her daughter Horatia, then 14, had to be spirited out of

*Blériot's plane*

*The moated citadelle*

Calais to avoid being held responsible for her mother's debts.

Lady Hamilton's death at No.111 rue Française, and her funeral, which was attended by the captains of all the English vessels lying in Calais harbour, was in many ways symbolic of the English characters who have flitted across the history of Calais.

Take, for example, George Bryan, as he called himself, who arrived in Calais the following year and settled in modest lodgings close to the harbour. His real name was George Bryan Brummel, or 'Beau' Brummel, the fop of the English court, who in 1805 had been sufficiently in royal favour to dine with the Prince of Wales on the Prince's birthday, at Brighton Pavilion.

But Brummel, whose wit left him a string of unrevenged enemies, ran out of friends and money and fled from England to escape his creditors. But the Prince always had a sneaking regard for him and, after he became George IV, threw him a lifeline when it was desperately needed. 'George Brummel is to be made Consul at Calais,' wrote Mrs Fitzherbert excitedly in December, 1827. 'The King has given his consent.' Actually Mrs Fitzherbert, the favourite and fattest mistress of the Prince of Wales, had got it wrong as usual. Brummel was eventually given the rather more modest post of vice-consul at Caen, in Normandy, in 1830.

**Lace making**

Many streets in Calais have British names – names like 'Edmund White', 'Robinson', 'Nottingham', and 'Bonington'. Bonington was a lace manufacturer in Nottingham, who after the defeat of Napoleon crossed the Channel in search of more promising outlets for his produce.

Lace factories survive to this day in Calais, with directors bearing English names, and elderly employees who lapse into English terminology when they have to explain the lace-making process. While the machinery is modern, lace-making has long since ceased to play a prominent part in Calais' economic prosperity, but the Musée des Beaux Arts et de la Dentelle in rue Richelieu has a number of interesting exhibits on lace and lace-making.

*Calais harbour*

## Artists in Calais

Bonington's artist son, Richard Parkes Bonington, was to play a role in the development of French Impressionist painting. As for English painters, they had been kept out of France during the Napoleonic Wars, and after Waterloo wasted no time in looking for new images across the Channel. Indeed, George Vincent, a painter of the Norwich School, was a passenger on that infamous first steamboat crossing by the *Élise* in 1816, when, according to his colleague John Berney Crome, he 'belched as loud as the steam packet'.

William Hogarth was another English artist who visited Calais with his sketch book. The year was 1748, when England concluded a particularly humiliating peace through the Treaty of Aix-la-Chapelle. On the morning following his arrival Hogarth was innocently, if tactlessly, to be seen copying an English royal coat-of-arms still visible on a pillar next to Calais' eastern gate, watched by an increasingly abusive crowd. When the guard turned up to see what the commotion was about, they arrested Hogarth as a spy and hauled him up in front of the local magistrates. Hogarth's indignant explanation that he was a professional artist with no interest whatsoever in military installations did not cut much ice with the French. He was incarcerated in Calais jail until some friends, hearing of his plight, greased a few French palms with English guineas. Hogarth was released, but only to be frogmarched down to the port and unceremoniously dumped on a fishing boat bound for Dover. Hogarth took particular exception to this, for he had already paid another skipper in advance to collect him a week later, and he never recovered his money.

Hogarth's reaction to his humiliation is clear in one of his most famous pictures, the 'Calais Gate'. It has a glimpse of the coat of arms he was sketching when so rudely interrupted, but its most prominent features are the townsfolk of Calais, dishevelled soldiers, ugly, gawping fishwives, and lascivious friars. A far cry from the friendly inhabitants of Calais today.

## Shopping

Calais has two main shopping areas: one is around the rue Royale, the other is centred around Boulevard Jacquard and Boulevard Lafayette in Calais Sud, the old village of St Pierre.

### Rue Royale district

*Maison de Fromage* more than 200 types of cheese; perhaps not Olivier's (see Boulogne), but worth a visit; it is in rue Gerschell, off Place d'Armes
*La Madrague* luxuries for the bathroom; posh household goods
*Outhier* cakes

*Au Gourmet* charcuterie
*Le Cellier* wine
*Etchola* household goods

### Boulevard Jacquard district

*Au Printemps* a department store (nationwide chain)
*Fin Bec* cheese and wine
*Prisunic* a department store (nationwide chain)
*Petyt la Cave* hardware
*Baby Comfort* clothes for children
*Cupillard* cooking utensils

Apart from food shops, most shops are closed all day Sunday and many are closed for part or the whole of Monday also.

### Markets

Place Crevecoeur, off Boulevard Lafayette, Thurs and Sat
Place d'Armes, Wed and Sat mornings.

### Hypermarket

'Le Continent' is in avenue Guynemer, 1½ miles east of Calais, well worth a visit. Its best sections are wine, cheese and kitchenware. There is a free bus service from the ferry terminal. If you avoid lunchtime, you can wheel your trolley into the crêperie bar for a splendid meal. Open 9am–10pm; closed Sun.

The largest supermarket is also a little way out of town,

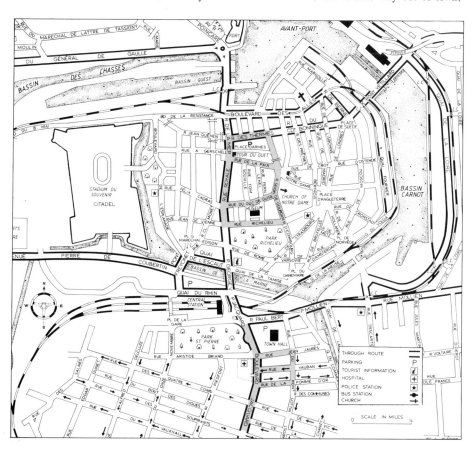

*The market in the Place Crevecoeur*

on the N43 to St Omer, called Prix Gros. Open 9am–noon, 2pm–7pm Tues-Sat; (3pm–9pm Fri) closed all Sun and Mon am. In the centre of town, try the GRO supermarket, 54 Place d'Armes, 9am–12.30pm, 3pm–7.30pm; closed Sun.

**Tourist Office**
12 Boulevard Clemenceau, Tel (21) 96 62 40 October – mid June: 9am–noon, 2pm–6.30pm, Mon–Sat; closed Sun. Mid June –September: 9am–10pm Mon –Sat; open on Sun in July and August.

**Opening times**
Museé des Beaux Arts et de la Dentelle (Museum of Fine Arts and Lace): 10am–noon, 2pm–5pm daily; closed Tues and public holidays.
Lighthouse: 10am–6pm July–late August, or ring (21) 34 35 69.
Musée de la Guerre (War Museum): St Pierre Park, May–September 10am–6pm. Closed rest of year.

**Parking**
No real problem in side streets, but watch out for mopeds parking in front and to the back of you, making it impossible for you to move.

**Changing money**
Bureau de change at ferry port (24 hours) and hoverport, but rates offered by banks much better. Several banks in Boulevard Jacquard, 9am–noon, 2pm–5pm Mon–Fri; a few banks open on Sat mornings.

---

**Accommodation**

---

**Hotels**
*Meurice*\*\*\* 5 rue Éd.–Roche, Tel (21) 34 57 03. The best hotel in Calais, the Meurice can trace its history back to an inn built nearby in 1772 by Augustin Meurice, when the only means of crossing the Channel was by packet boat (often a simple fishing boat carrying the mail). The Calais inn was the first of five on the way to Paris. Comfortable, quiet, very good value. The adjoining restaurant *La Diligence* is under different management, and you are not required to use it.

*Bellevue*\*\* 23 Place d'Armes, Tel (21) 34 53 75. Quiet, plain rooms, Continental breakfast only.
*Windsor*\*\* 2 rue Commandant-Bonningue, Tel (21) 34 59 40. English breakfast included, but no restaurant. Close to ferry terminal. Good value.
*Sauvage*\*\* 46 rue Royale, Tel (21) 34 60 05. Excellent service, comfortable rooms, interesting restaurant.
*La Capitainerie*\*\* quai du Danube, Tel (21) 96 10 10. Modern hotel close to ferry port. All rooms have bath.

**Restaurants**
*Le Channel* 3 Boulevard de la Résistance, Tel (21) 34 42 30. Difficult to beat for quality and value. Peer into kitchen to see what is cooking. Plush surroundings, packed with local French on Sunday at lunchtime. Good value. Closed Sun evening, Tues out of season and whole of December.
*Touquet's* 57 rue Royale, Tel (21) 34 64 18. Actually Calais' casino, where from 8pm–3am you can try your luck at roulette or blackjack. You can eat more or less all day from noon–2am if you can catch a waiter's eye. Food excellent, but conversation impossible. Closed Mon.
*La Côte d'Argent* Plage de Calais, Tel (21) 34 68 07. Very good for seafood, as one might expect, given its position. Used by the locals. Closed Mon, first two weeks in February and September; eves in winter.
*Au Coq d'Or* 31 Place d'Armes, Tel (21) 34 79 05. Good value, especially house wine. Closed Wed.
*Les Dunes* Blériot-Plage, Tel (21) 34 54 30. Another locals' haunt despite tourist location. Closed Sun eve and Mon.

# Dunkerque

Dunkerque is a child of the sea: until the seventh century it existed only as a sandbank lurking treacherously just below the water. But when the sea receded, a village grew up round the chapel founded by St Eloi in the dunes. By the 11th century, the word Dunkerque began to appear in French documents, meaning 'church of the dunes'.

Those shallow waters of Dunkerque, called the Banks of Zeeland, played their part in England's momentous struggle against the Spanish Armada in the summer of 1588. Dunkerque was at that time little more than a garrison town in the Spanish Netherlands for the huge army assembled by their commander, the Duke of Parma. For many months that year it had also been the scene of an incredible digging operation in which a second army, this time of Flemish workmen, had been mobilised by the Duke to carve out a canal between Dunkerque and Sluys, which remains to this day.

Parma needed his canal to move the 130 flat-bottomed ships he had assembled at Sluys to join another 70 at Dunkerque, the proposed transport for his army across the English Channel. The sea route was firmly shut, dominated by the Dutch fleet of small ships that had powerful guns but drew very little water. They could operate to the very edge of the sandbanks without running aground.

Despite years of planning the joint expedition against England, this simple yet fundamental flaw had been completely overlooked. The galleons of the Spanish Armada drew some 25 feet of water; the shoals off Dunkerque were safe only for ships drawing five feet or less. So, when the Armada fought its way up the Channel for the intended link-up with Parma, the plan was doomed from the start: the Armada could not go in, and Parma, for fear of being picked off boat by boat by the Dutch, could not come out. Indeed, in sailing as close to the Spanish Army as they dared, the Armada exposed themselves to English fireships, and to a wind that blew them closer and closer to destruction among the treacherous sandbanks off Gravelines and Dunkerque. It was only a sudden shift in the wind that saved the Armada from disaster, or rather postponed it until the ravages of the wild coasts of Scotland and Ireland.

Dunkerque, situated just inside the French border with

*The third largest port in France – Dunkerque*

*Place Jean Bart in 1900*

Belgium, has changed hands many times in the course of its history. The Spanish lost it finally in 1658, when a relief force, aiming to lift the combined siege of the English and the French, was defeated on June 4 at the Battle of the Dunes. Dunkerque subsequently surrendered to the English, who kept the town under the terms of the peace treaty. It was, however, but a brief possession. After the death of Cromwell, and the restoration of the monarchy, the new King, Charles II, was soon casting around for every conceivable source of money, anything rather than go cap in hand to Parliament. In May 1662, Dunkerque was sold to France for five million crowns.

**Pirate**

What must have seemed a good deal to Charles was less welcome to William and Mary, whose joint accession linked England and Holland against the French. In the twilight period that existed before outright war started, Louis XIV turned a blind eye to the activities of a notorious pirate, Jean Bart, who preyed on English and Dutch shipping from his Dunkerque base, taking or sinking more than 2,000 vessels before his death in 1702. Dunkerque remembers his exploits with a monument in the Place Jean Bart; the corsair was buried opposite in St Eloi church, which, together with the little street between the church and the town hall leading to the Place du Général de Gaulle, is all that survives of Dunkerque's past.

Until the outbreak of World War II, Dunkerque had retained much of the style of a 17th-century Flemish seaport, with streets and buildings of great charm and beauty. All that disappeared in the great evacuation from Dunkerque in 1940, an escape achieved, as the French are quick to remind us, through the courage of the French troops who had to stay behind. The beaches where British soldiers waded up to their necks, and paddle boats and pleasure craft braved German dive bombers to take them back to Blighty, lie to the east of the town in Malo-les-Bains and beyond.

The Dunkerque of today is a completely modern port (Dunkerque Ouest), the third largest in France. Giant oil tankers jostle for space with huge container ships and a multiplicity of smaller transports, moored alongside vast concrete acres of docks; huge cranes swing to and fro, while from the naval dockyard comes a ceaseless clatter of men and machines: truly rivetting. It is certainly not a pretty sight but it is an absorbing spectacle. You can tour the harbour by boat most days to see what is without doubt Dunkerque's greatest showpiece.

The port is a few miles west of the town itself, which has its own smaller harbour. The land between the two is in the throes of development from the original dunes and much of it is still little more than wasteland. The town, though no masterpiece of architecture, is a welcome relief. But the really pleasant part of Dunkerque is Malo-les-Bains, with its long, sandy beach perfect for games of every description, and an agreeable promenade. Only the sea wall is a reminder that this was once part of the Channel itself.

## Shopping

Dunkerque's shopping area is around the Place Jean Bart.

*Nouvelles Galeries* Boulevard Alexandre III, department store
*Au Sanglier* Boulevard Alexandre III, charcuterie
*Hossaert* rue Poincaré, bakers
*Boutteau* Place Jean Bart, pâtisserie
*Chorus* Place de la République, fashionware
*Sinclair* rue Wilson, milliner
*La Ferme* rue Poincaré, cheese
*Uniprix* Place de la République, department store
*Sophie* Pl. Jean Bart, perfume
*Mességué* Place Emile Bollaert, delicatessen

### Market
In the Place du Théâtre, Wed and Sat mornings.

### Hypermarket
The 'Auchan' hypermarket is 3 miles from Dunkerque on the N1, between the port and the town. Open 9am–9.30pm Tues–Sat; 2pm–9.30pm Mon; closed Sun. The Rond Point commercial centre at St Pol-sur-Mer also claims to be a hypermarket.

### Changing money
The main Tourist Office in Dunkerque (see right) has change facilities. The principal banks are to be found on Boulevard Alexandre III and in the Place du Palais de Justice, 9am-noon, 2pm–5pm, Mon–Fri. Changing money on Sundays in winter, other than the poor rate offered by hotels, can be a problem.

### Parking
For convenience for shopping, try Place Jean Bart; however there is more room in Place du Théâtre or Place de la Gare.

### Tourist Offices
The Belfry (Belfroi), rue Clemençeau, Tel (28) 66 79 21, 9am–noon, 2pm–7pm except Sun in winter.
Sea wall, Malo-les-Bains, Tel (28) 63 61 34, in high season.

### Opening times
Musée des Beaux Arts, Place Général de Gaulle, 10am–noon, 3pm–6pm. Closed Tues.
Musée d'Art Contemporain, 10am–7pm. Closed Tues.
from Bassin du Commerce, Tel (28) 69 47 14.

## Accommodation

### Hotels
*Frantel*\*\*\* Tour du Reuze, 2 av J-Jaures, Tel (28) 65 97 22.

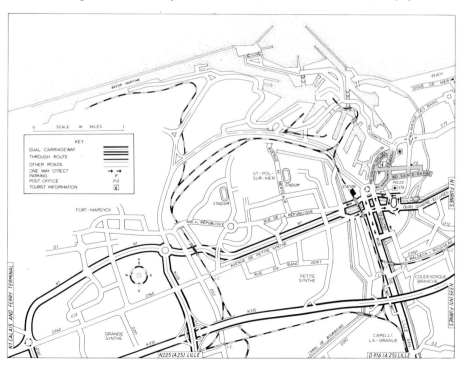

Modern hotel overlooking harbour; reasonable restaurant. *Europ-Hotel\*\*\** 13 rue du Leughenaer, Tel (28) 66 29 07. Largest hotel in Dunkerque; good service; easy parking. *Hirondelle\*\** 48 av. Faidherbe, Malo-les-Bains, Tel (28) 63 17 65. Very good value, especially the restaurant, which is closed Sun eves and all Mon and mid August – early September. *Metropole\*\** 28 rue Thiers, Tel (28) 66 84 18. Comfortable, but may be a little noisy; closed weekends.

**Restaurants**

*Richelieu* Place de la Gare, Tel (28) 66 52 13. Flemish cooking, and superb; conversation occasionally halted by the station announcements, but then this really is the station buffet. Puts British Rail catering to shame. Closed Sat and Sun evenings. Booking advisable, and don't expect to finish in time to catch a train. *Victoire* 35 av. des Bains, Tel (28) 66 56 45. Flemish cooking, delightful but expensive. Closed Sat lunch, Sun eve, and second half of August. *Le Mareyeur* 83 rue Henri-Terquem, Tel (28) 66 29 07. Seafood specialities, very good value. Closed Sun eves, all Mon.

# Environs of Boulogne and Calais

A map showing the part of Northern France within easy reach of Boulogne and Calais is on pp. 82–3.

## Dunkerque to Calais

### Téteghem
An obscure village barely three miles from Dunkerque on the D204, Téteghem is worth a visit simply to sample the outstanding cooking at La Meunerie restaurant, a 19th century mill. It is situated just south of the village on the D4. Extremely popular, so booking is more or less essential. Restaurant: *La Meunerie,* 174 rue des Pierres, Tel (28) 61 86 89. Closed Christmas–late January, Mon. also Sun eve and public holiday eves.

### Fort-Philippe
Where the Aa River reaches the sea, there are two old fishing villages, called Grand and Petit Fort-Philippe, named after the Spanish King, Philip II. Now seaside resorts for the impoverished French.

### Gravelines
Where Drake's fireships made the Spanish Armada scatter

*Little fishing ports and sandy beaches lie all down the coast*

*The white cliffs of Cap Blanc Nez*

and dissolve into chaos (see Dunkerque p. 77). But while only the rolling waves serve as a reminder of the unpredictability of the sea, the 17th-century fortifications are perfectly preserved. Like many others in northern France, they were the work of Sebastien de Prestre de Vauban, the French military engineer who flourished under Louis XIV when France was expanding her frontiers.

### Calais to Boulogne

**Sangatte**
Napoleon, having failed to break the English control of the seas, planned to build a tunnel to England from here, but thought better of it. A tunnel was finally started in 1877, but abandoned. When, or perhaps if, a new tunnel is constructed, Sangatte remains

a popular starting point, because of its proximity to Dover. A monument to the Dover Patrol, the British minesweeper fleet that kept the Channel open for British shipping during World War I, can be seen on the cliffs.
Restaurant: *Le Relais,* 919 Route Nationale, Tel (21) 85 05 51. Sea views, good value, rooms above. Closed Sun eves, all Mon, except mid June – end August.

**Escalles**
Closest place you can stay to **Cap Blanc Nez,** literally White Nose Cape, which is the highest point on these cliffs. A sight of the milk-white waves out in the Channel gives a clue to why this is known as the Opal Coast. Outstanding views.
Hotel/Restaurant: *L'Escale,* Tel (21) 85 25 09 (address not needed – find Escalles, and you

cannot miss it). Excellent fish-based menus, comfortable rooms, good value. Closed late September – end February except for Sunday lunches.

**Wissant**
Fine beach which, whatever they claim in Boulogne, may well have been the precise spot where Julius Caesar set off on his invasion of Britain.

**Cap Gris Nez**
Where the North Sea meets the English Channel, where the Channel swimmers are spurred on by their first sight of the French coast, and from where, on a clear day, you can pick out the fishing boats entering Boulogne.
Musée du Mur de l'Atlantique: former redoubt, now a museum on German fortifications of World War II. Open daily, for times Tel (21) 35 90 11 or 32 97 33.

# ENVIRONS OF BOULOGNE AND CALAIS

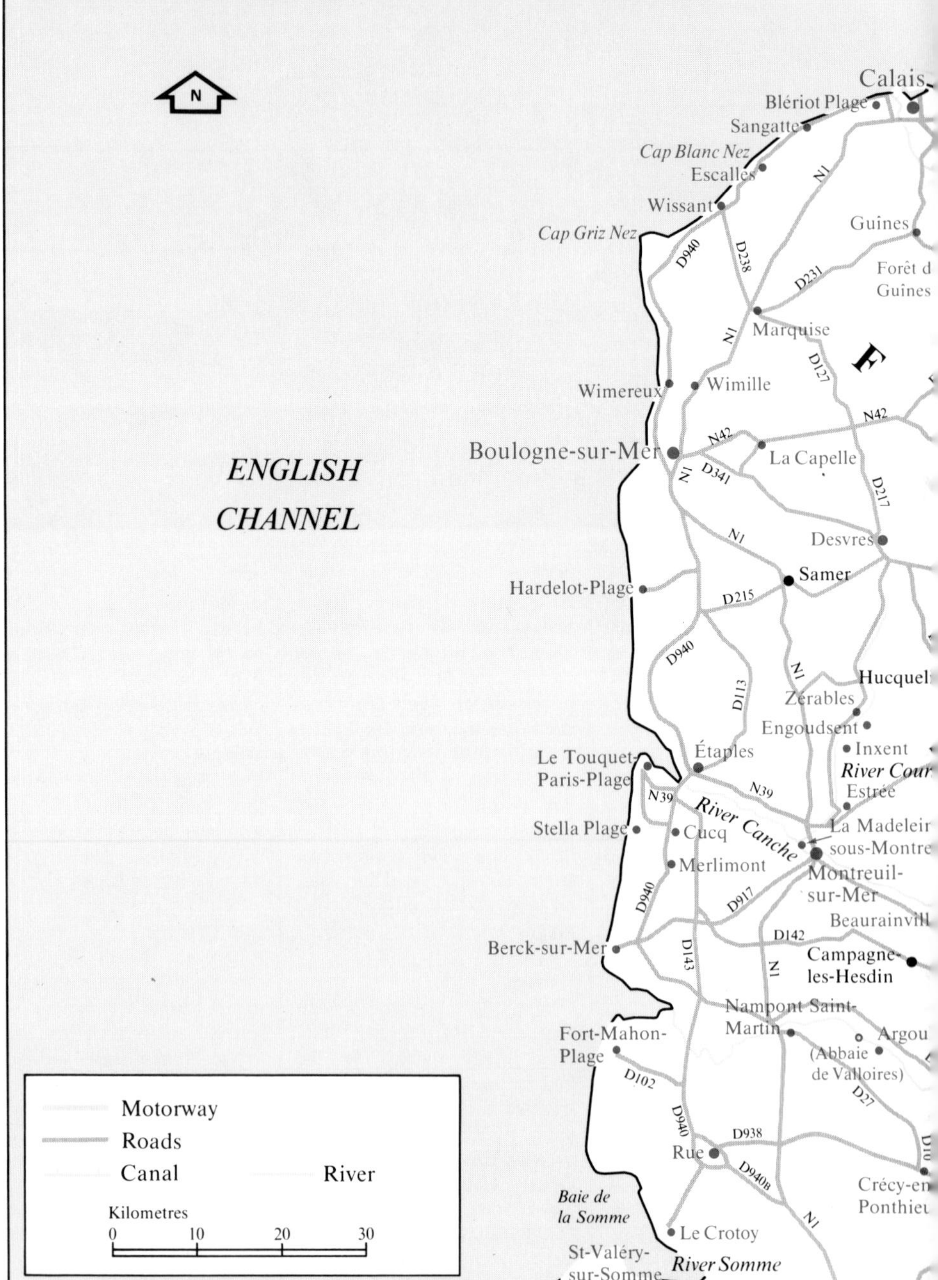

N

Calais

Blériot Plage

Sangatte

Cap Blanc Nez

Escalles

N1

Wissant

Cap Griz Nez

Guines

D940  D238

D231

Forêt d
Guines

N1  Marquise

D127

E

Wimereux  Wimille

N42

*ENGLISH*

*CHANNEL*

Boulogne-sur-Mer

N42

D341

La Capelle

D217

N1

Desvres

Samer

Hardelot-Plage

D215

D940

N1

Hucquel

D113

Zérables

Engoudsent

Le Touquet-
Paris-Plage

Étaples

Inxent

*River Cour*

Estrée

N39

N39

Stella Plage

Cucq

*River Canche*

La Madelein
sous-Montre

Merlimont

Montreuil-
sur-Mer

D940

D917

Beaurainvill

D142

Berck-sur-Mer

D143

N1

Campagne-
les-Hesdin

Nampont Saint-
Martin

Fort-Mahon-
Plage

Argou

(Abbaie
de Valloires)

D102

D27

D940

D938

D10

Rue

D940B

Crécy-en
Ponthiei

Motorway
Roads
Canal  River

Kilometres
0  10  20  30

*Baie de
la Somme*

N1

Le Crotoy

St-Valéry-
sur-Somme

*River Somme*

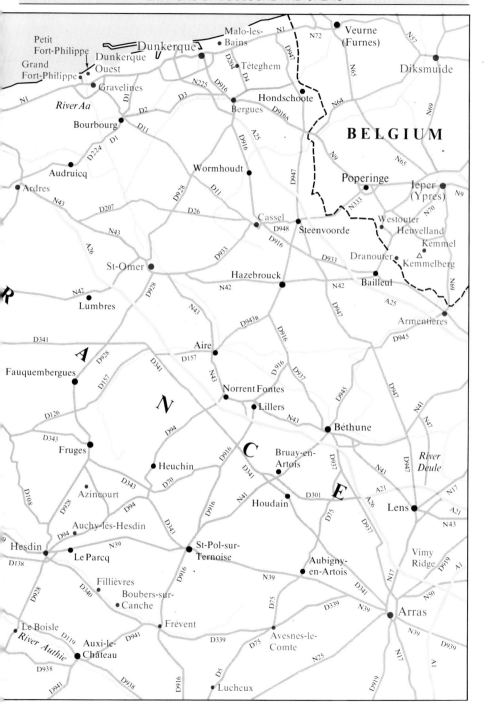

*Wimereux beach and promenade*

Restaurant: *La Sirène,* Tel (21) 92 84 09. Overlooks the sea, excellent fish dishes, very busy in high season.

**Wimereux**
A ghost promenade, the unexplained mystery of the Opal Coast. Apart from the famous Atlantic Hotel (see below), the sea front is full of abandoned, boarded-up houses and apartments; not a single shop, which must be unique. Yet in the last century, Wimereux was the height of fashion, the last stop on the tram line from Boulogne. Now it is left with its memories. The beach revealed by the receding tide has long stretches of hard sand and rock pools, to children's delight. For those who hate commercialism, sheer paradise.
Tourist Offices: Town Hall, rue Carnot, Tel (21) 32 46 29. During season, Place Albert I, Tel (21) 32 43 14.

Hotels: *Atlantic\*\*\** digue de la Mer, Tel (21) 32 41 01. Justly famous, though more as a restaurant, as it has only ten rooms. Spit-roasts a speciality, also fish dishes. The hotel is closed in February, the restaurant, Sun eves and all Mon October–March.
*Centre\** 78 rue Carnot, Tel (21) 32 41 08. Family run, friendly, on a main street. Restaurant packed with locals. Outstanding value. Restaurant closed Sun eves and all Mon November–March; hotel closed early June and over Christmas and New Year.

**Boulogne to the Somme**

**Le Portel**
Just south of Boulogne. Tiny resort, frequently overlooked – its main attraction. Sandy beach. Tourist Office: Place Poincaré Tel (21) 31 45 93.

**Hardelot Plage**
Magnificent beach, sweeping dunes, backcloth of pines and lakes; supposedly fashionable but lacking that intangible quality of Deauville and Le Touquet. Outstanding for golf, awful if you hate golfers.
Tourist office: Domaine d'Hardelot Tel (21) 91 91 00.
Hotels: *Regina\*\** avenue François I, Tel (21) 32 81 88. Excellent restaurant with fish specialities, but closed Sun eves and all Mon out of season. Hotel closed mid December–end January.
*Pré Catelan\** Tel (21) 32 70 03. Pleasant service, good value, but too many golfers. Closed October–end March.

**Etaples**
Fishing port in the Canche estuary, bustling atmosphere, and brightly painted little houses. Fish market in frenetic main square.

Hotel: *Lion d'Argent* Place Général de Gaulle, Tel (21) 94 60 99. Long rather than famous history, with nooks and crannies still sporting initials carved by British soldiers during World War I, when they were sent to convalesce in 'Eat Apples'. Promising restaurant, closed Tues.

**Le Touquet-Paris-Plage**
When flying across the Channel was *à la mode*, and motorists plucked up enough courage to drive their cars up the ramp and on to the Silver City aircraft at Lydd, Le Touquet was where they got off.

That was Le Touquet's second flutter with fashion. The first was back at the turn of the century, when the British in effect created the resort for their own personal convenience. The promenade, the teashops, the Westminster Hotel, were all there so that British holidaymakers could enjoy themselves without sampling anything that was remotely nasty and foreign. Almost literally, Le Touquet was a facade, like a film set, with buildings on only one side of the street. Behind the beach, arguably the best in France, the affluent classes sat snugly, and smugly, in their villas – built among the pine and birch trees, with names like Low Wood Manor, Anchorage, Lone Pine and Byways.

The names remain the same, but the owners are now largely French. It has finally become 'Paris-Plage'. You can see them arrive on Friday evening in their Peugeot Estates, after a frantic motorway drive from Paris, complete with children, dogs and even the au pair. They are going to enjoy themselves to the point of exhaustion, dash back to Paris on Sunday, and do it all over again the following weekend.

Le Touquet is at its best for night-owls and sportsmen. Golf and tennis are played with a fanatical determination, and a level of gamesmanship of which Stephen Potter would have approved; the same people, remarkably, seem to make up the clientele in the night clubs, dancing till dawn and beyond. In the summer, international stars appear at the Forest Casino. Shopping, too, in the chic boutiques, has become almost a religion, with customers pausing only to lament that a credit card that pays off all the other credit cards has still to be put on the market. The one bargain basement, Griffmode, close to the prom, has wild scenes of disorder, and changing rooms of such chaos that it is quite feasible to leave wearing someone else's underwear.

Tourist Offices. Hôtel de Ville, Tel (21) 05 27 55. Palais de

*Le Touquet in 1927*

l'Europe (seasonal), Place de l'Hermitage, Tel (21) 05 21 65. Hotels: *Westminster*\*\*\*\* av. du Verger, Tel (21) 05 19 66. No longer quite living in the grand manner, as nowadays it offers bed and breakfast only. But the rooms are all extremely large and comfortable. Closed November–Easter. 145 rooms. *Le Manoir*\*\*\* avenue du Golf, Tel (21) 05 20 22. Country house atmosphere, alternating between a thriller and a farce, ominous suits of armour cleaned by chambermaids in black dresses and white frilly aprons. Vast rooms, terrace, swimming pool, and, for golfers, an excellent golf course. Closed early January – early February. Restaurants: *Chez Pérard* 67 rue de Metz, Tel (21) 05 13 33. A shop as well as a restaurant, almost exclusively fish; superb dishes, great ambience, packed with French families on Sundays for lunch, when booking essential. Good value.

*Flavio* Club de la Forêt, av. du Verger, Tel (21) 05 10 22. Breathtaking fish specialities, breathtaking bill at the end, but worth it just to say that you have been there. Located between the Westminster Hotel and the Casino de la Forêt, which gives an indication of the average, well-heeled clientele. Closed January–February and Wed October–April.

**Stella Plage**
Just south of Le Touquet, and another fine beach with mile upon mile of sand. More seasonal than Le Touquet, as most hotels and shops close completely during the winter. Tourist Office: Boulevard Labrasse, Tel (21) 94 72 75. Hotel/Restaurant: *Sables d'Or* \*\* 1184 avenue de Concorde, Tel (21) 94 75 22. Just inland on D940 at Cucq. Simple rooms

but excellent restaurant with competitive prices. Closed end October–mid January.

**Merlimont**
On the D940; has a prodigious amusement park, Bagatelle, which attracts visitors from the length and breadth of France. Huge success with children, but note that it is open only between Easter and the end of September. In all 55 acres. Tourist Office: avenue de la Plage, Tel (21) 94 32 90. Restaurant: *Hostellerie Georges* 139 rue d'Etaples, Tel (21) 94 70 87. Still more fish. Closed January, Mon eve, all Tues, some public holidays – except in the peak season.

**Berck-sur-Mer**
Or Berck Plage, as it is sometimes called. Unless you like beaches, it has little to offer. Hordes of children during the school holidays, which may be why the owner of one hotel, the Comme Chez Soi, shuts during many of them. Tourist Office: in the town hall annexe, rue Casimir-Périer, Tel (21) 09 01 20. Hotel/Restaurant: *Le Trou Normand*\*\* 31 av. Tattegrain, Tel (21) 09 12 13. Excellent cheap, table d'hôte menus.

**Fort-Mahon-Plage**
Six miles of beach, but desolate out of season. Tourist Office: Place Bacquet, Tel (22) 27 70 75 (mid June– September only).

**Le Crotoy** See page 95.

---

### Arras to the Channel

---

Before the A26 motorway was built, British motorists would breathe a huge sigh of relief once they were past Arras.

Going south, they were well on the way to Paris; going north, only 75 miles, and St-Omer, lay between them and the Channel ports. As a consequence, few of them ever saw Arras as anything less than a blur or, if they followed the heavy goods route, barely glimpsed it at all. Now with the autoroute available almost to Ardres the pressure may sometimes be off, and visiting Arras and many other places broadly between there and the Channel can be a positive pleasure.

**Arras**
In the 17th century Arras was an important centre for the cloth trade. Its prosperity is reflected in the red-brick, arcaded town houses, which have been restored to their former glory, belying the damage inflicted on Arras in two World Wars. The two central squares, one leading into the other, Grand' Place and the Place des Heros, are the most perfect surviving example of the Flemish architecture of the period and the coats of arms of the craft guilds that paid for them to be built have been given their former pride of place. The Saturday market, famous since the 16th century, still continues as colourful and crowded as ever.

Beneath the ornate facades are deep cellars, from where the Resistance plotted during the Occupation. Another huge cellar nearby is full of wine bottles, more than 100,000 of them, which belong to the Restaurant Chanzy; some are more than 100 years old. The owner will take visitors around occasionally if asked, and a more formal tour of the honeycomb of underground passages starts in the basement of the Hôtel de Ville, with its lovely chiming belfry.

*Arras – 17th century magnificence*

Tourist Office: 7, Place du Mal-Foch, Tel (21) 51 26 95. Hotels: *L'Univers*\*\*\* 5 Place Croix-Rouge, Tel (21) 21 34 01. It scarcely seems possible that in bustling Arras you can leave the traffic and the crowds behind, but this former 18th-century monastery makes a wonderful retreat. It has 37 rooms, and an excellent restaurant.

*Chanzy*\*\* 8 rue Chanzy, Tel (21) 21 02 02. Modest hotel, graced by a superb restaurant, mostly Flemish cooking, and with huge portions. The wine cellar could reasonably claim to be among the best in France. Hotel never known to close.

Restaurant: *Ambassadeur*, Place Mal-Foch, Tel (21) 23 29 80. Michelin thought this station restaurant worthy of a rosette, and even by French station restaurant standards, it is quite magnificent. Train passengers hanging enviously out of the windows, have been known to ask their driver if he will come back for them in a couple of hours. Fish and grill specialities; you can eat almost to bursting point. Closed Sun eves.

### Vimy Ridge

Much of World War I was fought and re-fought over the same few miles of territory, with appalling losses on each side. None more so than at Vimy Ridge, between Arras

*The Canadian memorial at Vimy Ridge*

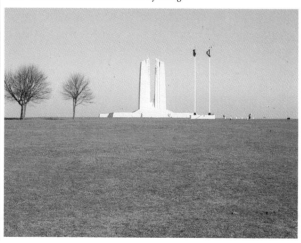

and Lens, where in April 1917 the Canadians attacked and pushed back the German positions. There is a monument here to the 74,000 Canadians who died fighting in France. A few rows of the trenches they dug to survive the German shelling have been preserved on the side of the hill: a place to stand and reflect.

## Lille

Many potential visitors are deterred by the fact that Lille is a huge industrial conurbation, but much of Old Lille has been restored and is well worth seeing, especially the rue de la Monnaie, home of what was one of Europe's earliest stock exchanges. In the Place de la République, the Palais des Beaux Arts is one of the finest in all France, with all the great schools of painting represented. Across the Deule Canal, the citadel is the largest and most perfectly preserved in France; needless to say, Vauban constructed it.

The River Deule once surrounded the city, hence its original name, L'Isle, the island. Ruled successively by the Counts of Flanders and the Dukes of Burgundy, Lille fell to Louis XIV after a nine-day siege in 1667 and has been French ever since.

Tourist Office: Palais Rihour, Place Rihour, Tel (20) 30 81 00.

Restaurants: Even the first class hotels in Lille do not have a restaurant, because they simply cannot compete with the best that Lille has to offer, including four that have won Michelin rosettes.

*Flambard* 79 rue d'Angleterre, Tel (20) 51 00 06. The house itself, late 17th century, is what in England would be known as a listed building; and the cuisine matches the superb setting – including outstanding turbot and sole terrine. Hugely expensive, but worth every franc. Closed early January, late July, August, early September; Sun eve, all Mon. Booking essential.

*Le Compostelle* 4 rue Saint-Étienne, Tel (20) 54 02 49. Another historic setting; this was a hotel as early as the 16th century. Fish specialities, incomparable service. Closed Sun eve.

*Paris* 52bis rue Esquermoise, Tel (20) 55 29 41. More splendid terrine, prodigious specialities, and the menu changes every two weeks, so you can never get fed up with the food. The chance to do so would be a fine thing! Closed early August-early September and Sun eve.

*A l'Huîtrière* 3 rue des Chats-Bossus. Tel (20) 55 43 41. Seafood is its speciality. Marvellous wines. Another restaurant which, as well as Sunday even-

*Cassel above the Flanders plain*

*Vauban's fortifications at Bergues*

ings, closes altogether from late July to early September, so visiting Lille for a gastronomic experience during the peak holiday season may prove a dismal failure.

**Armentières**
Remembered by the British for Red Rowley's music hall number:

> Mademoiselle from
> Armenteers, parley-voo.
> Hasn't been kissed for forty years, parley-voo.
> Mademoiselle from
> Armenteers,
> Hasn't been kissed for forty years,
> Hinky pinky, parley-voo.

During the Great War Armentières was always within a mile or two of the front and in the British sector until the Germans took it briefly in 1918. With most of their own menfolk fighting the war some-

where else, it seems a safe bet that some of the mademoiselles from Armentières did 'parley-voo'.

**Cassel**
On a clear day they say you can see four countries, France, Belgium, Holland and England, from this plateau above the Flanders plain. With its huge, cobbled central square, narrow sloping streets and crumbling staircases, Cassel has kept much of its 17th-century charm. On top of the hill is a statue to Marshal Foch, who had his headquarters here early in World War I. In 1940 Cassel was the scene of a fierce battle, when 2,000 thousand British troops were killed, holding off the Germans to cover the retreat to Dunkerque.
Restaurant: *Auberge de la Longue-Croix*, at Longue-Croix, south of Cassel on D138,

Tel (28) 41 93 34. A little difficult to find, but exceptional food at modest prices; fish specialities. Closed Christmas, January, Sun eves, all Mon and public holidays. Extremely popular, so reservations strongly advised.

**Bergues**
Only 5 miles south-east of Dunkerque, Bergues is quite the most picturesque town in French Flanders, with delightful old streets and canals, ringed by fortifications The northern side is protected by Vauban's formidable 'Couronne d'Hondschoote', a complex of concentric moats and walls.
Tourist Office: At the Belfry in the town centre, Tel (28) 68 60 44 (high season only).
Hotel/Restaurant: *Au Tonnelier*\* 4 rue du Mont-de-Piété, Tel (28) 68 70 05. Near St Martin's church, 12 rooms, but

*The quiet charm of St-Omer*

a first-class restaurant (sometimes closed Fri). The hotel is shut for the first two weeks in September.

### St-Omer

Another town for navigators to curse in the pre-motorway era, but now stopping by choice can be a delight. Saint Omer was a Benedictine monk who drained the marshes and founded a monastery, around which the town was built – until, perhaps rather ungratefully, the Benedictines moved out lock, stock and barrel more than a century ago, to the Château of Wisques close by. In St-Omer itself, the Cathedral of Notre Dame is a beautifully-proportioned basilica dating back to the 13th century. Ancient shops and cafés and neat little waterways adorn what has become a quiet country town.

Hotel: *Hostellerie St Louis* at Bollezeelle, 11 miles NE off D 928 , Tel (20) 68 81 83. An 18th-century manor house with log fires in winter; restaurant worth a visit itself. Closed early January – mid February. Restaurant: *Le Cygne* 8 rue Caventon, Tel (21) 98 20 52. Remarkable ambience in ancient building, with cooking to match. Duck superb, service also superb; outstanding value. Always busy: better to book. Closed most of December, Tues and Sat lunch.

### Ardres

Where you run out of motorway just before Calais, and could do worse than stop for a breather in the Grande Place, cobbled and cock-eyed, with crumbling old houses all around that look in need of support.

Hotel: *Grand Hotel Clément\*\*\**, Place Maréchal-Leclerc, Tel (21) 35 40 66. Family run, and like most families, has the occasional off-day, but it is a charming hotel, just the same. Its restaurant is outstanding, but not cheap. Hotel closed mid January-mid February; restaurant closed most Sun eves, Mon and Tues lunch.

### Guînes

On the road from Ardres you pass near Guînes Forest and the Field of the Cloth of Gold, where Henry VIII met François I of France; but anyone hungry enough to try one of the few roadside cafés should remember that the two kings brought their own catering. Guînes, itself, has a little square with sleepy dogs and old men sitting in the sunshine, unchanged in half a century and full of atmosphere.

Hotel/Restaurant: *Lion d'Or* 7 Place Maréchal-Foch, Tel (21) 35 20 51. Logis de France, comfortable, cheap rooms, excellent restaurant. Very good value. Closed 2nd half September.

**Marquise**

On the N1 between Calais and Boulogne, but the market square escapes the worst of the traffic and offers a surprise: an old coaching inn, complete with a traditional courtyard, called *Le Grand Cerf*. British visitors with little French but considerable imagination suppose it was named after some clodhopping yokel who kept sloshing the soup over the boots of the English milord; and they could be right.

Hotel/Restaurant: *Le Grand Cerf*\* 32 avenue Ferber, Tel (21) 92 84 53. Several menus, all good value; restaurant packed with locals. Closed Sun eve and all Mon.

---

### Maigret Country

Many of the television episodes from Georges Simenon's stories of a French detective were shot in Hesdin, a tiny town which is ideally suited for exploring a largely unknown part of France of great beauty less than half a day's drive from the Channel ports. The Canche and Authie river valleys, winding in a leisurely way through woods and meadows, brushing tiny hamlets with whitewashed houses, offer an enchanting glimpse of a France where time has almost stood still.

**Hesdin**

The sharp accordion gathering pace, an Englishman posing perfectly as Maigret, the French detective, and striking an unstrikable French match on a grey, unwashed wall – the indelible memory of a tele-vision series that, paradoxically, killed Rupert Davies' acting career (because he and Maigret became inseparable in the eyes of the public) and made Simenon a best seller in England as well as France. For some years Hesdin, with its steep hump-backed bridges crossing the many rivulets that flow from the Canche and the Ternoise, had its peaceful existence interrupted each summer by the clapperboard and the paraphernalia of a film crew; until the stories ran out.

Hesdin is still Maigret country, with little mysteries behind the lace curtains of its Renaissance houses, and conversations that stop in mid-stride when a stranger passes on the way to the market square. Yet the history of Hesdin is stranger still, with a town hall that was once the palace of a Hungarian princess. She was Marie, sister of Charles V, the Hapsburg Emperor who in the 16th century founded Hesdin as a fortified outpost of his dominions to guard the crossing of the Canche River. When the French finally managed to dislodge the Spanish inheritors of the Hapsburg empire, it was at the expense of the belfry of the Church of Notre Dame; it was

*Hesdin*

demolished by a stray artillery shot and hideously rebuilt.

Tourist Office: Hôtel de Ville, Place d'Armes, Tel (21) 06 84 76.

Hotel: *Trois Fontaines*** 16 Route d'Abbeville at Marconne, on the outskirts of town. Tel (21) 86 81 65, A Logis de France hotel, friendly, comfortable, with quiet rooms. Restaurant closed Fri and Sun eves, except at the height of the season.

*Des Flandres*** 22 rue d'Arras, Tel (21) 86 80 21. Atmospheric hotel in the centre of town, but restaurant may not always be consistent. Good meals are, however, very good indeed. Closed late December–mid January.

*La Chope** 48 rue d'Arras, Tel (21) 86 82 73. Unpretentious rooms, outstanding French and Flemish cuisine. Advance booking essential in peak season. Restaurant closes on Fridays in winter months.

### Auchy-lès-Hesdin

Slightly to the north-east, with a church containing the tombs of many of the French knights killed at the Battle of Agincourt on October 25, 1415. Agincourt, or Azincourt, lies to the north just off the D 928 to Fruges. A simple cross commemorates the battle in which an exhausted English army under Henry V, 10,000 men of whom many were too ill to fight, defeated the full might of the French nobility, perhaps three times their number. You can still see the boggy fields and the wooded copses where the French knights were caught in a funnel, floundered in the mud, and were cut down by the English long bow and nimble English foot.

### Fillièvres

Seven miles along the Canche, south-east of Hesdin, an exquisite village covered with flowers during the summer. A former watermill is a charming place for a meal or a night.

Hotel/Restaurant: *Auberge du Vieux Moulin**, Tel (21) 04 83 42. Bar packed with locals, pleasant rooms, good cooking, including trout from the river Canche. Open all the year round.

### Boubers-sur-Canche

Three miles further still, busy little village, more flowers, more people. In the village square, try:

Restaurant: *La Cremaillère,* Tel (21) 04 20 03. The locals' bar as well, friendly if slow, food excellent. Closed Tues, except for drinks.

### Pommera

Drive through Frévent, past the 18th-century Château de Cercamp, cross the Canche, then take the D339 to the 16th-century church at Avesnes-le-Comte. Afterwards, south by back roads, to:

Restaurant: *La Faisanderie,* Tel (21) 48 20 76. A converted farmhouse with outstanding fish specialities. Closed most of February and August, Sun eves, all Mon; prices are reduced in midweek. Booking strongly advised. La Faisanderie is easier to find from Doullens as it is four miles north-east on the N25 in the Arras direction.

### Doullens

Another Vauban fortress on the River Authie, a testimony to the man's amazing industry, helped, of course, by the almost unlimited resources of Louis XIV, his master. From here the D938 runs along the north bank of the river, past Lucheux and the ruined castle of the Counts of St Pol; at Le Boisle, noted for its basket weaving, the road becomes the D119 and then, crossing the Authie, the D192 to:

### Argoules

A charming little village with a huge lime tree in the centre of the green, which presumably gave its name to the *Auberge du Gros Tilleul*. There is, however, an even better place to stay:

Hotel/Restaurant: *Auberge du*

*In the valley of the Canche*

*Montreuil's ancient cobbled streets*

*Coq en Pâté*, Tel (22) 29 92 09. Tiny rooms but excellent country cooking. The telephone switchboard came out of an old mine and still works. Very good value. Restaurant closed Friday, but the patron still cooks for hotel guests.

Further along the D192 is the Abbaie de Valloires going back to the 12th century, but now a children's home, and Nampont-St-Martin, another small village on the river, with a fine 15th-century fortified mansion whose moat was fed by the River Authie. From there, a traumatic experience, north on the noisy N1 a few miles to:

### Montreuil-sur-Mer

Don't waste time looking for the sea – it has not been to Montreuil for centuries, but this was once the navigable limit of a much wider estuary. Montreuil, overlooking the left bank of the River Canche, remains a supremely picturesque place. Its 700-year-old ramparts are intact and can be circumnavigated in an hour's walk, which will be rewarded by breathtaking views over the countryside. You have Vauban to thank for their survival, as he practically rebuilt the town and what Vauban built, stayed up. In the citadel is one of the earliest rolls of honour, a list of the local lords who fell at Agincourt, emphasizing what a disaster that battle must have been for the nearby communities, whose whole livelihood depended on the patronage of the local knights. Montreuil's narrow, cobbled streets lead into tiny tree-shaded squares, which, alas, are packed with tourists in the summer. To sample the real atmosphere, hope for a sunny day in early spring or late autumn.

In the Place Général de Gaulle there is a statue of Earl Haig who had his headquarters in Montreuil during World War I. A lively market happens here too.

Tourist Office: Place de la Poissonnerie, Tel (21) 06 04 27, high season only.

Hotels: *Château de Montreuil* \*\*\* 4 Chaussée des Capucins, Tel (21) 81 53 04. An elegant, if comparatively modern, château quietly situated with a lovely garden and stupendous, breathtaking food. Only 12 rooms, but all well furnished. Expensive, but worth it. In high season, booking essential – but there are special deals at quieter times of year. Closed mid December–mid February; restaurant also closed some lunchtimes.

*Auberge la Grenouillère* at La Madeleine-sous-Montreuil, Tel (21) 06 07 22. A mile or so outside Montreuil, down a narrow lane beside the River

Canche. This was once a series of farm labourers' cottages, now converted into a splendid auberge. Rooms plain but comfortable, outstanding food in classic French style; à la carte only. Closed completely in February; restaurant closed Tues eves and all Wed out of season.

## Valley of the River Course

North of Montreuil, in the direction of Desvres, is the Vallée de la Course, a beautiful yet startlingly peaceful district, so well hidden, that even French tourists have not properly discovered it yet. Every village, it seems, has a promising place to eat and drink:

### Estrée

Not to be confused with Estrelles, on the opposite bank, a rival since the Wars of Religion, when they took opposite sides. *Relais de la Course,* Tel (21) 06 18 04, river fish specialities, as you might expect, comfortable rooms, open all year.

### Inxent

The river flows beside its main street, where you find the *Auberge d'Inxent,* Tel (21) 06 86 52, an old cottage restaurant. Increasingly fashionable among knowledgeable locals, so prices going up; but it offers excellent traditional French cooking. Closed mid September–mid October, Mon eves, all Tues, except occasionally in July and August. Booking advisable.

### Engoudsent

A tiny hamlet, with a bar-café-restaurant called *Au Bon Accueil,* Tel (21) 90 70 63, which offers meals only at lunchtimes. Superb value, but increasingly busy at weekends.

### Zérables

Finding the village is easy enough, but to find *Cocatrix-Grémont,* Tel (21) 90 73 39, which describes itself as a café-restaurant, turn off down a cart track just before, marked, discouragingly, Auberge, which it isn't. The restaurant, none too tastefully decorated has views over Lac d'Amour and exceptional fish dishes.

### Beaurainville

After returning to Montreuil by the same route, take the D113 north of the river towards Hesdin, skirting the edge of the forest. At Beaurainville is an undistinguished-looking inn that hides an outstanding restaurant, the *Val*

*On the River Course*

*de Canche\**, Tel (21) 90 32 22. Comfortable rooms, excellent food, very good value. Closed Christmas, Sun eve and all Mon (except occasionally).

## Valley of the Somme

### Crécy-en-Ponthieu

A tiny town in Picardy north of the Somme, and south-west of Hesdin. A cross records the fact that on a hill close by, on August 26, 1346, an English army of some 10,000 defeated at least twice that number and killed more than 1,300 French knights, the flower of their nobility among them. Edward III, who spent most of the

*The cross which commemorates the battle of Crécy*

battle as a prudent spectator watching from the top floor of a windmill, had coached his archers and knights to become a skilled combination, and this was perhaps the first joint battle action by yeomanry and aristocracy in war. The knights by and large fought dismounted, darting in and out of the chaos of massed ranks of Frenchmen and frantic horses, already hit by a hail of arrows, to administer the coup de grâce. Edward III's son, the 16-year-old Prince of Wales, won his spurs in a series of heroic charges, while Jean of Luxembourg, the blind King of Bohemia and brother of the French King Philip VI, ordered himself to be tied to his horse during the battle, and, inevitably, was slain.
Hotel/Restaurant: *Le Canon d'Or* 10 avenue de Général-Léclerc, Tel (22) 29 51 14. This is a delightful old post inn, with huge beams and, in winter, a roaring log fire. Excellent local dishes, especially fish, and comfortable rooms. Closed in January and many weekends in winter.

### Rue

Like Montreuil, a sea-port in the Middle Ages, but now left high though not exactly dry in the marshy coastal plain between the Authie and the Somme. It offers wild life in abundance, including, at Marquenterre on the coast, an interesting bird sanctuary. The Chapelle du St-Esprit has superb 15th and 16th century stonework.

### Le Crotoy

On the north side of the Somme estuary, outstanding centre for sailing, ideal for hardy bathers on windswept beaches. Shell fish in abundance, sent all over France. Hotel/Restaurant: *La Baie\*\** address simply Le Crotoy, Tel (22) 27 81 22. Delightful rooms overlooking the bay, but essential to book ahead. Closed most of January. Its restaurant *Chez Mado*, deservedly famous, superb cuisine, booking vital.

### Saint Valéry-sur-Somme

The dyke, built to keep back the sea on the south side of the estuary of the Somme, is also a splendid promenade. Tiny port, splendid ramparts, plenty of atmosphere in summer, but bleak and deserted in winter. Restaurant: *Les Pilotes* 62 rue de la Ferté, Tel (22) 27 50 39. Good value. Closed December, January and Wed except in peak season.

If you have plenty of time, follow the course of the Somme, beautiful scenery, south east past Abbeville some 30 miles to:

### Amiens

One of the most beautiful cathedrals in France, and indisputably the largest, makes Amiens worth a visit, however great your aversion may be to sprawling cities, which Amiens undoubtedly is. Inside the cathedral are 126 pillars, outside a spectacular spire and a lavish frontal facade decorated with magnificant statues. Restaurant: *Petit Chef* 8 rue Jean-Catelas, Tel (22) 92 24 23. Outstanding for regional cooking. Closed first half of February, second half of July, Sun eve and all Mon.

# Ostende

Though it may sometimes be a little difficult to credit it now, in the 1880s it was as chic to spend a summer holiday in Ostende as on the French Riviera. Ostende, after all, was the western terminus of several versions of the Orient Express, and travelling even by Pullman to eastern Europe was so arduous, that many passengers prepared for the journey with a few days in Ostende, and recovered there again on the way back. Ostende's casino was crammed every night, not just with young English bloods hoping to mitigate their debts across the Channel; but also by Parisians, spending their ill-gotten gains free from awkward questions from the French tax authorities.

### Sea bathing

The British not only made the first use of the seaside for recreational purposes, they also exported the idea to the Continent, though not without some initial resistance from the natives. When Tobias Smollett, who could reasonably be regarded as the earliest travel writer, swam in both the Channel and the Mediterranean in 1763, some horrified doctors regarded him as a lunatic and diagnosed imminent death. In the days when plumbing was non-existent and washing extremely rare (and ladies wore perfume to kill off more unpleasant smells), the idea of actually volunteering to go in the sea seemed insanity itself.

Yet catch on it did, and among the Channel resorts, Ostende made most of the running before World War I. Its initial visitors were invalids,

*Ostende beach and the Europanorama building*

for doctors were beginning to appreciate that the healing properties of sea-water compared quite favourably with those of hot springs or mud baths. Jules Janni said of the scene at Ostende in the summer of 1833 that there were so many ill and deformed Englishmen in the water, accompanied by nurses and some even by their doctors, that it was a 'quite hideous sight'. Charity to the sick was not a strong point of the age. Dr Arthur Granville, reporting that the Channel resorts were attracting invalid custom even from Prussian Germany, observed that the invalids were lured there 'for the dubious benefit of sea-water and instead of dying from their ills, they were dying of boredom'.

Ostende had a lot going for it if you were an Englishman in search of, well, titillation. In early Victorian England the sexes were rigorously segregated anywhere near the sea, but in Belgium mixed bathing was in full swing by the 1850s. It was still, of course, done in a seemly fashion – at Ostende an excited British visitor reported that the ladies bathed holding their parasols above their heads, but, oh the scandal of it, 'never unaccompanied by gentleman escorts'.

The Belgian Channel resorts were also much better organised than most in France or England. The local hotels had acquired territorial rights over long stretches of sand, and while the practice of paying to use the facilities, as happens now in some parts of the Continent, had not yet crept in, hotel staff were employed to keep the beach clear of pedlars and general riff-raff, to spare the guests annoyance. Their material comfort was also well cared for, with wooden boards laid in lines from the prom-enade to their beach parasol, and additional coconut matting to the water's edge.

The hoteliers of Ostende were not content with deck chairs, an invention of P & O on their voyages to Egypt in the early 1880s; many had ordered wicker chairs from Madeira in such quantities that visitors to the island complained of a sharp rise in prices. For a while the new chairs did not catch on, which did not surprise the editor of *Holiday Haunts*, Bernard Becker. 'They have every virtue, it is true,' he wrote, 'but they not only shelter, but conceal the occupant. What, I should like to know, is the use of a delicious seaside toilette if madam is to be buried in the vast arms of a porter's chair? What becomes of the killing costume and the scarlet umbrella if they are literally put under a bushel?' What Mr Becker had yet to receive by way of intelligence, or perhaps he had not interpreted its true

significance, was that Ostende had suddenly adopted *double* wicker chairs. They were now infinitely suitable for goings on that made the concealment of the occupants not a handicap, but a positive advantage.

Stripes were in, too, towards the end of the nineteenth century: striped tents, striped bathing costumes, even striped canvas-topped bathing huts, that lay threateningly by the water's edge like some hideous war machines mounting an invasion.

It was World War I that brought the golden age of Ostende to a premature conclusion. Using the plan devised by Count von Schli-effen ('Let the last man on the right brush the Channel with his sleeve'), Germany swung wide to avoid the main French armies, and on October 15, 1914, took Ostende. It remain-ed in German hands for four years and three days, never out of artillery range of the front. Ostende, including its beaches, was a shambles, full of barbed wire and booby traps.

However, the port's days as a fashionable resort had already been numbered. The train and the car had cut the time it took to reach the south

of France down to a day or two at the most, a far cry from the 16-day journey experienced by Smollett in the 18th century. What is more, sun bathing caught on in a big way in the 1920s, and the bright young things no longer regarded the Riviera as a place to go in the winter, but arrived in summer, lay in the sun and swam in the Med. Ostende simply could not compete.

### Family holidays
Instead, Ostende sensibly decided to concentrate on the growing business of family holidays. Its hotels went up in numbers, to almost 200, but down in amenities and, more important, down in price. Its casino concentrated less on attracting millionaires and more on star entertainment, still a feature in the present day. The sandy shoreline remains the queen of the Belgian beaches, but now has an emphasis on family activi-ties, such as sailing and wind-surfing, There are snack bars in abundance, and no shortage of ways to amuse children. A miniature train, running on the road, tours the town; the marine aquarium is out-standing; and for those with

*Fashionable Ostende in 1905*

a good head for heights, Europanorama is, at 340 feet, the tallest building on the Channel coastline. From the rooftop restaurant the views over the Channel can be quite breathtaking on a clear day.

## Carnival time

If a weekend is what you want, the first one in March should not be missed. For this is when the Ostende Carnival takes place, and the town goes mad – almost everyone made up as a clown, lantern processions, fireworks, and a giant bonfire. The famous Casino Ball, has the slightly unprepossessing title of 'Le Bal du Rat Mort'. Tickets include dinner, and deceased rodent is definitely not on the menu. The ball's name actually comes from an 1890s Parisian night-club of infamous reputation. It attracts an incredible 5,000 guests, who dance to six orchestras until dawn.

## Shopping

Most of the important shops are concentrated in the streets leading from the central square, the Wapenplein:
*Casa* Adolf Buylstraat, linen and household goods
*Trois Suisses* Kapellestraat, knitting wool
*Intersport* Hendrik Serruyslaan, toys
*Chopin* Adolf Buylstraat, cakes to eat or take away
*Leonidas* Kapellestraat, chocolates

Fluent English is spoken in almost all the principal shops. Clothes, especially haute couture and there for children, are outstanding in design, but rather expensive by British standards.

## Markets

Wapenplein, Thurs mornings, more modest version Mon and Sat for food and clothes; Sun morning, for flowers.
Langestraat 67, for antiques; days vary. Ring first on (059) 50 10 18.

## Hypermarket

Ostende does not possess a hypermarket, but it has two supermarkets, the Maria-Jose, in Adolf Buylstraat; and the Delhaize, in Leopold II laan, much the bigger of the two.

## Changing money

Bureau de change available at the ferry terminal, 6 am–7.30 pm in peak season, but unfavourable rates. Most banks are open 9 am–12.30 pm, 2 pm–4.30 pm; some to 8 pm on Fridays. On Saturdays during the summer season, 9 am–noon.

## Parking

For convenient access to places and shops of interest, park on the Groentemarkt, or Wapenplein, but on Mondays, Thursdays and Saturdays, severe restrictions apply before 4 pm.

## Tourist Office

Feest-en Kultuurpaleis, Wapenplein, Tel (059) 70 11 99 or 70 60 17. Mid September to May: 8am–noon, 1.45pm –5.45 pm weekdays, 9am–noon, 2pm–5pm Sat; closed Sun. June to mid-September, Easter, Whitsun: 9am–1pm, 2pm –8pm Mon-Sat, Sun and public holidays 10am–1pm.

## Opening times

Museum of Fine Arts, Wapenplein: 10am–noon, 2pm–5pm daily, closed Tues and all October.
Provincial Museum of Modern Art, Romestraat II: 10am–

noon, 2pm–5pm daily, closed Tues. More than 1000 works of art on display.
Mercator Three-master Museum, old yacht harbour: opening times vary enormously but 10am–noon, 1pm–4pm Sun out of season, 9am–7pm daily in season should find it open.
North Sea Aquarium, Visserskaai: 10am–noon: 2pm–5pm all weekends, all April and May; daily, June-September.
Europanorama, Van Iseghemlaan 7: 10am–7pm daily.
Miniature train: 10am–6pm, city tour from Seamen's Memorial, Easter, Whitsun, weekends June & September, daily in July & August. Tel (059) 32 44 30.
Wellington Race Course: from May-September, trotting races are held, sometimes under floodlights.

## Accommodation

### Hotels

Of the 101 hotels given official approval – and there are many more that have no official recognition – very few are on the Promenade, which may tell us something about the weather in mid-winter. For hotel reservations Tel (059) 80 33 15 or 50 06 60 during Tourist Office opening hours. After that you are on your own.
*Imperial*\*\*\*\* Van Iseghemlaan 76–78, Tel (059) 70 54 81/2 or 70 23 56.
*Prado*\*\*\*\* Leopold II laan 22, Tel (059) 70 53 06. Continental breakfast only. Modern, situated in pleasant square.
*Andromeda*\*\*\*\* Albert I Promenade, 60, Tel (059) 50 68 11. On the seafront. Exceptional bedrooms.
*Ambassador*\*\*\* Wapenplein 8A, Tel (059) 70 09 41/2/3; central, comfortable, and

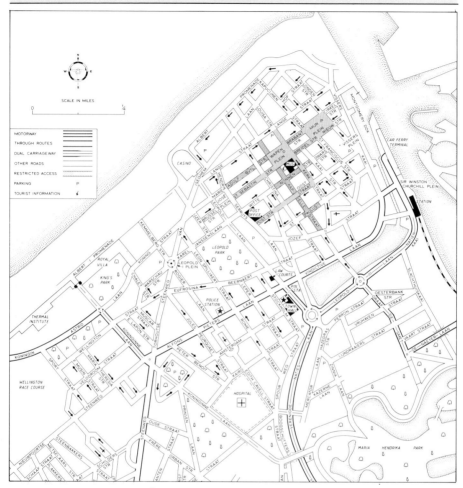

guarantees a parking space if you book a room.

*The Admiral* Langestraat 72, Tel (059) 70 86 56 or 70 66 66. Comfortable, good value; perhaps too many other Brits in the dining room.

*Die Prince* Albert I Promenade 41, Tel (059) 70 65 07 or 70 91 85 Modest public rooms, but well-furnished bedrooms; sea views.

### Restaurants

*Hostellerie Bretonne* Vindictivelaan 23, Tel (059) 70 42 22. Outstanding fish restaurant, whose specialities include hot oysters in champagne. Money has to be no object.

*Prince Charles* Visserskaai 19, Tel (059) 70 50 66. Not an evening to economise, but the meal is still worth it.

*Lusitania* Visserskaai 35, Tel (059) 70 17 65. Located on the quayside, and with a name like that the owner must have a sense of humour, or no knowledge of recent history. Quayside views, splendid lobster bisque soup, big portions of everything.

*Café Gloria* Albert I Promenade 60, Tel (059) 70 68 11. Linked with Hotel Andromeda (see hotel list), North Sea *bouillabaisse* outstanding.

*Le Grillon* Visserskaai 46, Tel (059) 70 60 63. Good value. Closed Thurs.

*La Crevette* Visserskaai 46, Tel (059) 70 21 30. Long history of outstanding cuisine. Closed 20 December and Thurs except peak season.

*Kwinte* Visserskaai 28 Tel (059) 70 13 43. Closed Wed.

*Hoeve* Visserskaai 27, Tel (059) 70 26 77. Closed Mon. Outstanding value.

# Environs of Ostende

A map of Western Flanders is on pp.102–3.

**De Panne**

A delightful resort between the sand dunes, despite the daunting statistics of more than 5,000 holiday flats available for rental and 37 hotels. The road from France, for de Panne is barely across the border, bisects spectacular rolling dunes that shelter a marvellous nature reserve, a paradise for walkers. That the dunes have survived the ravages of wind and tide is due largely to the foresight of Maurice Calmeyn, who in 1903, decided to try to hold together the sand by planting trees in it. His skill was such that 230 acres are now covered by the Calmeynbos (Calmeyn Wood), and no fewer than 25 varieties of trees have survived.

De Panne's hard, flat, sandy beach is perfect for sand yachts, whose history goes back to medieval times. The first was built by Simon Stevin of Bruges, and there are records of sand yacht races at de Panne since the beginning of the century. It is a spectacular sport, with modern-day machines capable of speeds of up to 75 mph; their flapping sails and screaming, clattering wheels, echoing against the sound of the wind and the surf, are an unforgettable sensation.

Behind the resort, at Adinkerke, is the Meli-park, a paradise for children with fairyland characters, games and amusements guaranteed to keep the little horrors out of mischief for the entire day. Back on the beach, many of the tourists have their heads down, not through disillusionment at their surroundings, but looking for shells: de Panne beach is a treasure trove of shells of many different kinds brought in by the tide.

Tourist Office: Town Hall, Zeelan 21, tel (058) 41 13 02 and 14 13 04. October-Easter: open Mon-Sat; Promenade, Tel (058) 41 29 63. Easter, then June-September: open daily.

**Koksijde**

Really three resorts in one, Koksijde, Sint-Idesbald and Oostduinkerke, forming one seaside community. Koksijde probably had the earliest settlement on this west coast of Flanders, with its 'Duinenabdij', the Abbey of the Dunes, founded by the Cistercians in the 12th century. The Abbey, an outstanding and fascinating medieval site, is open to visitors.

Koksijde has also been the traditional home of artists, with Paul Delvaux, the renowned surrealist painter, setting up a studio in the resort. Many of his major works are displayed in a special museum.

Further along the beach, Oostduinkerke is both an historical and living study of fishing folklore. The history is to be found in the National Fishery Museum, complete with many examples of ancient fishing craft. The living are the last mounted fishermen in Europe, who ride out into the sea carrying huge fishing baskets, dredging the wet silt in search of shrimps and prawns. How long the men and their mounts can continue this arduous life, no one knows: already there are only half a dozen survivors keeping up a way of life as old as Flanders itself. The shrimps they collect are superb, and you can try them for yourself in De Peerdevischer, a bar next to the Fishery Museum. In June, the

*Sand yachts*

mounted fishermen head a parade in the annual Shrimp pageant, a homage to their skill and the sea.

Tourist Offices: Town Hall, Zeelan 24, Koksijde, Tel (058) 51 63 42 or 51 63 75, weekdays only.

Infodesk Casino, Koksijde beach, Tel (058) 51 29 10, daily during tourist season.

Infodesk Sint-Idesbald, Koninklijke Baan 330, Tel (058) 41 39 99, Easter and July-August.

Town Hall, Oostduinkerke, Tel (058) 51 11 89; weekdays only.

Infodesk Oostduinkerke, Astridplein, Tel (058) 51 13 89, Easter and mid-June to mid-September.

Opening times: Abbey of the Dunes, 9am–6pm in season, 9am–12.30pm, 1.30pm–5pm out of season.

National Fishery Museum: 10am–noon, 2pm–6pm daily.

Paul Delvaux museum: 10.30 am– 6.30pm daily; April–September: 11am–5.30pm weekends only October–December. Closed rest of year.

### Nieuwpoort

A water enthusiast's paradise, with miles of sandy beaches, windsurfing and sailing. A huge marina stands next to the fishing port, from where fresh fish are delivered all over Flanders. Fish is, needless to say, the predominant offering on the menu at Nieuwpoort's quayside restaurants. Nieuwpoort stands on the River Ijzer, and in summer a delightful daily excursion operates along it as far as Diksmuide. For hardier sailors, a converted coaster offers a three-hour sea excursion three times a week along the Belgian coast. Although the ship is called the Jean Bart IV, after the famous corsair, the prices

*The mounted fishermen of Oostduinkerque*

suggest that there are no modern pirates on board.

Tourist Offices: Town Hall, Marktplein 7, Tel (058) 23 55 94. September–June: open Mon–Fri, Sat mornings, closed Sun. July and August: open Mon–Sat and Sun mornings.

Infodesk Nieuwpoort beach, Henrikaplein II, Tel (058) 23 39 23. Open Christmas, Easter and mid May–mid September.

River trips: contact A. Baert, Elisalaan 6, Nieuwpoort.

Sea trips: contact Vieren Company, Albert I laan 90.

### Middelkerke

Another example of two resorts in one, Middelkerke and Westende, and of mile upon mile of sandy beach. Inland, behind the 7,000 apartments for rent (you have been warned), are some delightful little polder villages – the polders being, as in Holland, land reclaimed from the sea – with white farmsteads, such as

the Schoorbakkehoeve on the Ijzer. During World War I the land between them was flooded to keep back the German advance. In the centre of Middelkerke is a concrete reservoir badly constructed in the 19th century and left with a violent tilt. It is called the 'Dronkenput' because visitors returning from a local bar sometimes convince themselves on seeing it that they have had one drink too many.

Tourist Offices: J. Casselaan 4, Middelkerke, Tel (059) 30 03 68, open daily June–September, closed at weekends rest of year.

Infodesk, Middelkerke Promenade, Tel (059) 30 33 94, July and August only.

Infodesk, H. Jasparlaan 173, Westende, Tel (059) 30 20 85. Easter, Whitsun, July and August only.

### Bredene

The survival of Bredene

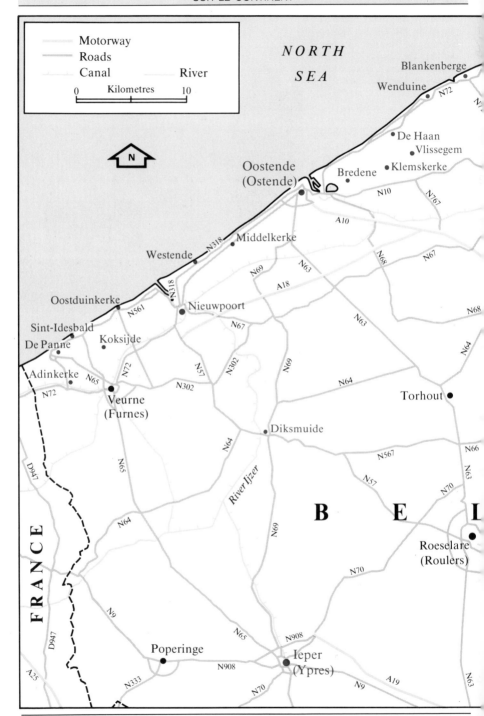

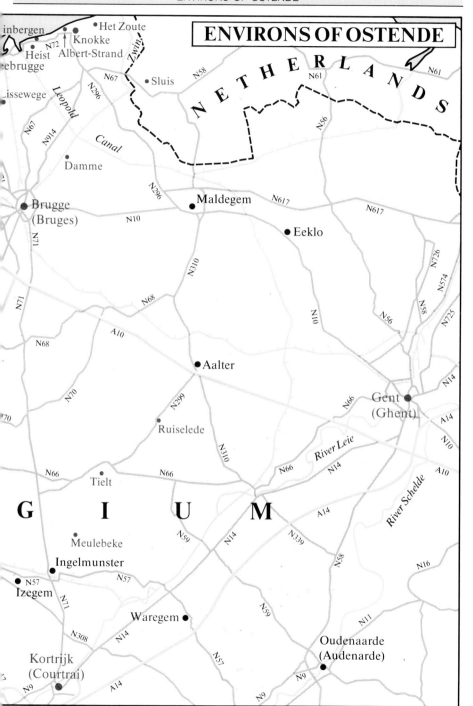

ENVIRONS OF OSTENDE

depends on a constant battle with the sea, which every year threatens to wash away the dunes that are the very basis of its existence. This is a popular area for campers, within easy reach of both Ostende and Bruges, ideal for children. In nearby Zegelaan, the Turkey-enhof Museum has a prodigious collection of North Sea shells.

Tourist Office: Infodesk Driftweg, Tel (059) 32 09 98.

### De Haan-Wenduine

A charming, sophisticated resort with splendid hotels and elegant villas, blended into spectacular, wooded dunes, stretching almost to the water's edge. On the first Saturday in August each year De Haan has the 'Trammelant', literally, the Festival of the Noisy Tram, so-called because trams used to rattle into the town every few minutes carrying holiday-makers. The quaint tram station has been preserved as a tourist attraction.

Wenduine, a small fishing village, has something of a mystical character. It was supposed to be the home of the Flanders giants, Louw, Pol de Kruwer, Scuteman and Wanne, figures from early folklore, who are remembered in an exhibition in the Town Hall. There is an exceptional view from the 'Spioenkop', the highest sand dune in Wenduine, from where the wives of the fishermen used to watch for their husbands' safe return. At Molenhoek is a marvellous animal park, while Klemskerke and Vlissegem are two delightful polder villages.

Tourist Offices: Town Hall, Leopoldlaan 24, De Haan, Tel (059) 23 57 23, weekday mornings only.

Infotourism De Haan-Centre Tramstation, Tel (059) 23 34 47, June and first half of September, open mornings only; Easter, Whitsun, July and August, open daily, and all day.

Infotourism, Wenduine Tramstation, Tel (059) 41 24 69, May, open mornings only; Easter, Whitsun, June – mid-September, open all day.

The Wenduine Giants: Town Hall, Wenduine, Mon-Fri 9am–noon.

Restaurant: *Le Coeur Volant*, Normandielaan 24, De Haan, Tel (059) 23 35 67. Sea food specialities superb; not for those on a budget.

### Blankenberge

The British can hardly fail to feel at home here. Blankenberge has a pier worthy of Southend or Margate, complete with the inevitable posse of fisherman dangling their rods hopefully off the sea end; bathing huts, many constructed during the last century; and the 'paravang', an exotic windbreaker in wrought iron, where you can huddle on blustery days and still enjoy the sun. Cars are kept well away from the beach, making a stroll along the Zeedijk, with its countless tiny terraces, an agreeable experience; you may still risk being run down, though, by one of the countless pedal cars, driven by budding little Grand Prix drivers at a ferocious speed.

Blankenberge has its own brand of Belgian cuisine, with the regional fish dishes a speciality; they come inevitably with 'frites', for Belgium chips are claimed (by the Belgians) to be the best in the world. Criticising Belgian food is always a delicate matter, roughly equivalent to casting aspersions on a Spaniard's manhood, and not to be undertaken lightly. When a Belgian is sticking up for his rights he

*Blankenberge's sands and pier*

is said, in Flemish, to be 'defending his beefsteaks'. Fortunately, in Blankenberge, this does not pose too much of a problem.

If you should eat too much, Blankenberge offers a quite unique way of exercising. On the promenade near the pier, is the Lustige Velodroom, the cycling equivalent of crazy golf. Its bizarre cycles can be used by all the family on its even weirder wooden track. Elastoplast essential.

Tourist Office: Leopold III Square, Tel (050) 41 22 27 and 41 47 01. Open daily in season; mid September to Easter, closed Sun and public holidays. Lustige Velodroom: open Easter to mid-September.

### Knokke

Actually five beaches in one, Heist, Duinbergen, Albertstrand, Knokke and Het Zoute, more than seven miles of glittering sand packed at the height of season by the widest possible range of holiday-makers, from impoverished campers to snooty Germans who rush down the motorway to stay in their private villas. Once the great trade ships passed here from Damme down the Zwin, but all that is left of their route is an exquisite nature reserve and bird sanctuary, ideal for walkers in wellingtons.

Knokke has an annual Festival of Humour, a kind of comedians' graveyard, and a cartoon museum whose collection is strengthened annually by exhibits from the World Cartoon Exhibition, held each year on Laguna Beach. Donald McGill would have loved it.

Tourist Offices: Info-Lichttorenplein Zeedijk, Knokke, Tel (050) 60 15 16.
Info-Heldenplein, Tel (050) 51

20 59, open public holidays, July and August.

Hotel: *The Links,* Elisabethlaan 69, Tel (050) 61 14 73. As one might expect, adjoins an excellent golf course. Quiet, comfortable, good service. Open all year, including Christmas, when there are special festivities.

Restaurant: *Aquilon,* Lippenslaan 306, Knokke, Tel (050) 60 12 74. Michelin accolades, outstanding fish-based cooking. Booking essential. Closed Sun eves, and other times when the owner feels like it.

### Ghent

Although to get to Ghent you have to cross from West Flanders into East, the motorway system in Belgium is such that it remains a quite practical proposition for a weekend visit by way of the Belgian Channel ports. See, at sunset, the three great towers of Ghent ranged one behind the other from St Michael's Bridge, and for that unforgettable view alone the effort will have been well worthwhile.

The city claims, with some justice, to have more historic buildings than Bruges and almost as many canals – crossed by more than 200 bridges. Much of its magnificent architecture came from the funds of the weavers, culminating in Cloth Hall, all Gothic splendour. But not quite as splendid as the towers of Ghent – the Belfry, next to Cloth Hall; the Church of St Nicholas; and St Bavo's Cathedral. Bavo, the patron saint of Ghent, was converted by Saint Amandus after an earlier career as a highwayman. He was said to be of noble birth, which makes the comparison with Robin Hood surprisingly close.

Ghent's turbulent history has its English connections. It was the birthplace of John of

*The castle of the Count of Flanders at Ghent*

Gaunt, fourth son of Edward III; John never inherited the English throne but was the ancestor of a line of Lancastrian kings, Henrys IV, V and VI. Also from Ghent was John of Cleves, whose unfortunate and ugly daughter, Anne of Cleves, became Henry VIII's fourth wife in January, 1540. It was a marriage based entirely on a misleading portrait and Henry divorced the lady he described unflatteringly as 'the Flanders mare' six months later.

Ghent has a reputation for doing nothing by halves. In its Belfry is one of the largest bells in the world, called Roland, itself the replacement for an even larger bell destroyed by Emperor Charles V. On top of the Belfry sits a golden dragon, 12 feet in length, appropriated by the Emperor Baldwin in Constantinople on his return from the Crusades. It cost the lives of several men in raising it 300 feet to the top.

In Ghent, too, the great cannon known as 'Mad Meg' was made in the 15th century. It is 17 feet long, weighs over 16 tons, and fired cannonballs weighing 750lb, although none too accurately according to contemporary accounts. It has not been moved from its present site since 1578, which in view of its size is perhaps none too surprising.

Beneath the Great Hall is a medieval torture chamber, with many relics of Ghent's cruel and violent past. The Ghent 'collar' is believed to have been invented here, an iron collar lined with razor-sharp spikes and placed around the prisoner's neck so that if he failed to keep his head upright, the spikes pierced his neck.

*Ghent's Guild Houses*

The castle was built by the first Count of Flanders, the splendidly named Baldwin of the Iron Arm, to deter raids by the Normans. Secure beneath its walls, the people of Ghent developed a flourishing cloth industry, until it was threatened by the Industrial Revolution in England, and in particular by James Hargreaves's 'Spinning Jenny'. In 1805, the newly-invented weaving equipment was smuggled across the Channel and found its way by mysterious means ... to the city of Ghent.

Tourist Offices: Dienst Toerisme, Borluutstraat 9, Ghent, Tel (091) 25 36 41. Open every day during the season.

Federatie voor Toerisme in Oost-Vlaanderen (East Flanders Tourist Federation), Koningin Maria–Hendrikaplein 64, Tel (091) 22 16 37.

Hotel: St Jorishof, Botermarkt 2, Tel (091) 23 67 91 or 2. Built in 1228, and retaining much of the original structure, the St Jorishof has a strong claim to be the oldest surviving hotel in Western Europe. It also has an excellent restaurant, closed Sun eves.

**Tielt**
Windmill country, with two in the town and a dozen more in the surrounding villages, silhouetted against the landscape. The most interesting to see are 'Knokmolen', at Ruiselede, built of stone in the mid 19th century; and 'Herentmill', at Meulebeke, with the longest flight of windmill steps in Belgium.

Tourist Office: Town Hall, Tramstraat 2, Tielt, Tel (051) 40 10 11. Mon–Fri, office hours only.

Herentmill: Open on request only. Tel (051) 40 03 67.

**Kortrijk (Courtrai)**
The National Flax Museum is situated here in a converted farmhouse, showing how flax was made in the days when this was a key to the prosperity of Flanders. Outside the town is a monument identifying the spot where for the first time foot soldiers defeated knights in armour and the French Army was cut to pieces by the combined forces of Bruges and Ghent on July 11, 1302; the fallen knights were stripped of their golden spurs. Eighty years later, however, at the Battle of Westrozebeke, another French army plundered Kortrijk and removed most of the spurs from the Church of Our Lady, where 700 had been hung up in triumph. There is no Flemish monument to that battle.

Tourist Office: Town Hall, Grote Markt 54, Tel (056) 22 00 33. Mon–Fri in winter; also Sat and Sun mornings during July and August.

National Flax Museum: open November–February: weekends 2pm–6pm; March–October: daily 9.30am–noon, 1.30pm–6pm.

**Ieper (Ypres)**
It says a great deal for the ramparts designed by Vauban, that they survived even the artillery bombardments of World War I, when Ypres remained the one pocket of Belgian territory held by the British, at the terrible cost of 55,000 lives. Every evening at eight o'clock, the Last Post is still played in their memory; a reminder, too, of the enduring futility of war.

Ypres has been rebuilt, so it takes a keen imagination to recreate the scenes of devastation around the town, which was often within range of the

German guns. Scarcely a single building of the town was left intact, and there are dozens of military cemeteries in the surrounding district. In the Cloth Hall is the Salient Museum, with vivid pictures from the Great War.

Tourist Office: Town Hall, Grote Markt 1, Tel (057) 20 26 26 and 20 26 23. Open daily April–September. Closed weekends, Mon afternoons and public holidays during the rest of the year.

Salient Museum: April –October: 9.30am–12.15pm, 1.15pm–5.30pm. Other periods by prior arrangement only.

**Heuvelland**
See map pp.82–3.
Not a place but a district, the 'heuvelland' or highland region, with three small towns, Dranouter, Westouter and Kemmel. Although far from being real mountains – the highest point, the Kemmelberg, is just over 500 feet high – the area has marvellous scenery and is ideal for a walking holiday. The village of Westouter, barely a mile from the French border, has a cable car and panoramic views. You can stay at the top of the Rodeberg, almost as high as Kemmelberg, and eat a gastronomic dinner, safe in the knowledge that you really can walk it off the following day.

Tourist Office: VVV Westvlaamse Bergen, Streekhuis Malegijs, Kemmel, Tel (057) 44 47 10.

Hotels: Kosmos***, Rodebergstraat 53, Westouter, Tel (057) 44 44 55 or 44 46 38. Fine service; good facilities.

'T Hof Zannekin Rodebergstraat 41, Westouter, Tel (057) 44 40 64. Unpretentious, no rooms with bath, but very good value.

*Zeebrugge, now a major port*

## Zeebrugge

For a ferry port, it seems ironic that Zeebrugge's principal claim to fame should be its closure. For on St Georges' Day in April, 1918, during World War I, the port was shut to shipping by the sinking of block ships in what Winston-Churchill described as 'an episode unsurpassed in the history of the Royal Navy'. Eight Victoria Crosses were awarded in an action that lasted barely 80 minutes. The raid, of quite reckless daring, bottled up dozens of German submarines for the next several months, a feat that had been beyond the Royal Navy's surface fleet operating in the Channel. Although its effect on the final outcome of the War is doubtful, the attack took place at the end of a period of major German advances on the Western Front, and was a great boost to morale.

The long curving mole, now extended to take even bigger container ships, was constructed between 1896 and 1907 to protect the entrance to Zeebrugge's docks from the prevailing westerly winds. At the time it was a prodigious engineering feat that eventually turned the quiet little fishing harbour of Zeebrugge into Belgium's third largest port, behind Antwerp and Ghent.

Zeebrugge is a mole, a lock and a dock – literally 'Bruges-on-Sea', as it was created by the burghers of Bruges, together with its canal, after Bruges' natural access to the sea had become permanently silted up. Bruges is a bare five miles away, and it would be a rare visitor to Zeebrugge who did not also visit Bruges.

However Zeebrugge is a seaside resort in its own right, with a small sandy beach, and beyond it, in the direction of Blankenberge, miles and miles of dunes with little ponds and lush greenery, a bird-watchers' paradise. Zeebrugge itself has five hotels and every conceivable water activity, an open-air swimming pool, a miniature golf course, tennis courts, and for those on sailing holidays, berths in the harbour for over 100 yachts. The truncated tower of Lissewege, with its fine views over the whole port, is also worth a visit. From here you can see that for all its modern industry, the heart of Zeebrugge survives in its 130-strong fishing fleet, whose catch is hauled ashore and auctioned off in the harbour, just as it was centuries ago.

## Shopping

The principal shops in Zeebrugge are on Brusselstraat, Kustlaan and Zeedijk. However, as the road from the ferry terminal leads directly to Bruges by the N298, only five miles distant, most visitors go there, a journey of no more than 20 minutes by car. The fish market in the harbour takes place on Monday, Tuesday, Wednesday and Friday.

### Tourist Office

Infodesk, on promenade close to start of main road to Bruges. Tel (050) 54 50 42. Open Easter and Whit holidays, weekends in June and September, daily in July and August.

### Opening times

Swimming pool 'Maritime', Brusselstraat. Tel (050) 54 52 67. Open early April–end September.
Midgetgolf, Duinpad. Tel (050) 54 52 67. Open April–mid September.
Lissewege, Tower of the Church of our Lady: open April 1–September 30, 9.30am–5pm.

## Accommodation

### Hotels

*Maritime\*\*\*\** Zeedijk 6, Tel (050) 54 40 66, (050) 54 42 24
*Monaco\*\*\** Baron de Maerelaan 26, Tel (050) 54 44 37
*de Pier\** Zeedijk 4, Tel (050) 54 44 83
*Strandhotel* Zeedijk 14, Tel (050) 54 40 55
*Thalassa* Zeedijk 16, Tel (050) 54 40 55 (as Strandhotel)

### Restaurants

*Asdic* Rederskaai 27, Tel (050) 54 60 56.

All the hotels in Zeebrugge have restaurants, of which the Maritime restaurant is the best, and, as you might expect, the most expensive.

# Bruges

The Common Market began not in Brussels in the twentieth century, but in Bruges in the fourteenth. For Bruges (Brugge in Flemish) was the dynamic centre of a trading association known as the Hanseatic League, whose members, not to put too fine a point on it, set out to acquire a trade monopoly by fair means or foul. If you wanted to buy or sell timber, pitch, tar, turpentine, copper, iron, livestock (everything from horses to hawks), salted fish, leather, hides, wool, grain, medicines or many textiles in Northern Europe, you had to deal with the League directly or offer them a percentage of your profits.

Although the Hanse had centres in London and such unlikely places as Bergen and Wisby, Bruges was the most ardent champion of Hanseatic unity. If you belonged to the League, you were virtually above the law and relieved of almost all taxes. Which explains why the wall decorations in Bruges' Town Hall, depicting events of historical importance, painted by the Flemish artists Albert and Juliaan de Vriendt, include a scene in which the town council renews the privileges of the Hanseatic League.

With its access to the open sea down the river Zwin, Bruges became the central clearing house of European trade, and its stock exchange, or *bourse*, regulated for the

*The Procession of the Holy Blood passes the Town Hall*

*Bruges' belfry stands sentinel above the canals*

first time the rates at which national currencies were exchanged throughout Europe. When the French attempted to reduce the dominance of Bruges by force of arms, they were beaten by the men-at-arms of Bruges and Ghent at the Battle of Kortrijk (Courtrai) in 1302 and suffered heavy losses (see p.107). Two of the heroes of this battle, Pieter de Coninck and Jan Breidel, live on as statues in Market Square. The triumphant return of the warriors of Bruges is

another scene in the wall decorations in the Town Hall.

Towering above the Market Square is the Belfry, built between the 13th and 15th centuries, although its carillon of 47 bells was not installed until 1743. If you sit outside a café in the square, you can hear them playing a different tune every quarter of the hour. These days they are played automatically, but for centuries playing them was an honourable and well-paid profession. Bruges still has its official carilloneur,

who plays on the bells three or four times a week, a mixture of old and popular melodies. Sunday is the best day to hear them, around midday, when traffic is comparatively light.

**City of Squares**
Bruges is a city of quite marvellous squares. Scarcely have you left Market Square, when you come into the Burg, with its unique collection of architectural styles. The Burg was built by the first Duke of Flanders, Baldwin I, around

110

870, when it consisted of a moated castle, a prison and a chapel. Today, apart from the gothic Town Hall, it contains the 16th-century Recorder's House, the Provost's House, the Court of Justice and, most famous of all, the Basilica of the Holy Blood.

When the body of Christ was washed before burial by Joseph of Arimathea, drops of the blood-stained water were said to have been kept by the followers of Jesus, and handed down from father to son. The relic of the Holy Blood was given to Derreck of Alsace, Count of Flanders, in 1150 by the Patriarch of Jerusalem, to mark his bravery during the Second Crusade. Contained in a small crystal phial with a golden stopper attached by silver chains, the relic was brought back to Flanders by the Count's chaplain. Each Ascension Day the phial is carried on a golden reliquary at the head of a solemn, yet spectacular, procession. At the front come girls in flowing blue cloaks singing the *Veni Creator,* followed by tableaux depicting biblical scenes and finally the golden shrine of the Holy Blood. In each window on the procession route burns a single candle.

Whatever one's views on the authenticity of its contents, the phial has undoubtedly had a charmed life. Hidden from the Germans in two World Wars, and earlier from the French during the time of the Revolution and the Napoleonic Wars, and still earlier from the Calvinists, it had its greatest escape during the 14th century. Bruges was attacked by Ghent, whose soldiers threw the phial into the river. Three days later one of the sisters in the beguinage saw the phial reflecting the light of the sun, just below the water level, and it was rescued. It can now be seen in the Basilica.

The beguinage was the home of beguines, the widows, unmarried sisters and daughters of knights killed in the Crusades and who, as a result, could no longer fend for themselves. Although they devoted a good deal of their time to charitable works, they were far from being nuns, or from being shut away from the outside world. Yet the beguinage, entered from a humpback bridge through a quaint gateway, is a startling contrast to the bustling centre of Bruges. Its little white houses and beautifully manicured lawns instill a sense of peace and contentment.

**Outstanding museums**

No tourist should be content without visiting the best of Bruges' outstanding museums. The city's picture gallery, built on the site of an old abbey, is the Groeninge Museum. It houses some of the masterpieces of the Bruges School of painting, including many works by Jan Van Eyck, who settled in Bruges. His painting of Canon van der Paelen goes into such spectacular and painstaking detail that where

*The peace of the beguinage*

*City of canals*

the Canon is depicted reading from the Bible using his pince nez spectacles, you can read the magnified words without difficulty. A less appetising picture by Gerard David, the last great master of the Bruges School, is also on display – a man being skinned alive, 'The Slaying of Sisamnes'. David painted it on commission from the burghers of Bruges, during their struggle against the Hapsburgs, when it was hung in the Court of Justice – a reminder, perhaps, of the penalties for treason, and of the fact that propaganda is not entirely a modern concept.

The works of another great artist, Hans Memling, are hung in St John's Hospital. Memling, wounded in France,

was cared for at the hospital, and painted during his convalescence. Particularly exquisite are the six miniatures painted on the side of a shrine and depicting the life of Saint Ursula, which must have taken Memling months of concentrated work.

In the grounds of St John's Hospital is a medieval pharmacy, where time seems to have stood still for centuries. A huge pestle and mortar for grinding powders, ancient scales, hundreds of tiny wooden drawers, all indicating that prescriptions did not fail the recipient through lack of preparation. One cupboard is set apart, still locked shut with an enormous key, and marked, as it was long ago, 'Poisons'.

During the conflict with the Austrians, the contents of this cupboard were sometimes used for purposes other than to keep down rats and mice.

Another museum not to be missed is the Gruuthuse Palace, where the medieval life of Bruges is best preserved, with displays of how the townsfolk lived at the time. There are sumptuously decorated and furnished drawing-rooms and bedrooms, and kitchens clanking with the implements of medieval cuisine, looking more like instruments of torture.

Further paintings of the Bruges School can be seen in the Church of Our Lady, including one of the most famous, David's 'The Transfiguration'. It is surpassed only by Michelangelo's bust of the Virgin and Child, which stands in a marble niche on the altar in the southern nave. Nearby, are two famous tombs, of Charles the Bold, one of the most famous of the Burgundian kings, and of his daughter Maria, who died in an accident while hunting wild boar.

## Canals and bridges

But the true treasure of Bruges is its complete ambience, its narrow streets, its gabled palatial houses and vivid architecture of many contrasting styles, testimony to its power between the 12th and 16th centuries. Bruges was then one of the most important cities in northern Europe, with, at its height, a population of more than 200,000. Its canals and waterways may not quite match the intricate elegance of Venice or the sweeping magnificence of Stockholm, but they are an eloquent expression to its charm and character. Bruges has more than fifty canal bridges, and these, coupled with its narrow, cobbled streets, represent too great a challenge for all but the most determined motorist. Better to abandon the car, and be taken on tour by horse-drawn carriage or canal boat.

The canals were once the life-blood of Bruges, in the days when big ships could sail up the Zwin as far as Damme, three miles from the city. As the name suggests, only by building great banks on either side of the river were the fierce winter tides of the North Sea kept back. It was on June 24, 1340, that a great naval battle was fought at Sluys at the mouth of the Zwin, by which Edward III won mastery of the seas from the French, and went on to beat them even more decisively at Crécy.

Yet, fifty years later, the Zwin was already showing signs of silting up, and despite frequent attempts to dredge it, the channel eventually closed completely, marking the end of Bruges' access to the sea, until the canal was built to Zeebrugge. Damme was left with its past, and with its eels, once a swarming delicacy of the Damme canal. Fresh eel

*See Bruges in comfort from a carriage*

has become rare, but in Damme, they can still show you ten different ways to cook them.

Belgium struggled successfully to free itself from the Dutch, but Flemish, a tongue similar to the Dutch language, remains the native tongue in many of the provinces. Some Flemings will not acknowledge French but will be more than happy to converse with visitors in English. Friction between the Flemish-speaking and French-speaking provinces seems likely to last, producing the apocryphal story of the rival sets of workmen sent to fill in the same hole in the road marking the linguistic boundary. The Walloons built their little hut and put up a sign which said 'We speak French here'. The Flemish built their little hut and went one better with a sign which said simply: 'And we work here.'

### Familiar words

Despite such semantic differences, Belgium has produced several words we take for granted in English. It is almost unheard of, for example, to eat any variety of sprouts other than Brussels sprouts; our children keep their playing kit and all kinds of rubbish in a duffel bag – which were once made only in the town of Duffel; Spa, where the Belgian royal family took the waters in the 18th century, now means any place with a healing spring. Then there is the Shrove Tuesday carnival at Binche, near Mons, which has a battle with fruit so violent that shopkeepers board up their windows before the procession starts. Belgium's Binche has become the British 'binge', a not entirely unfamiliar happening in some Channel ports.

### Shopping

Clean pavements and narrow shops are regular features in Belgium. Shopkeepers are responsible by law for the frontage outside their shops, and before they open each morning, regularly wash down the pavements. Shops are narrow because many are converted houses dating back to a period when taxes were determined on the width of a house. As a consequence, many Bruges homes are extremely slim, with rooms leading from one to another with no corridor space. Individual small shops remain commonplace, and stay open late at night.

The principal shopping streets in Bruges all lead into the Market Square, the Markt – Hoogstraat, Steenstraat, Geldmunstraat, Ezelstraat and Vlamingstraat. Shopping arcades, or 'galeries', originated in Belgium, and car-free shopping precincts are common.

Among the best Belgian products are chocolate, crystal, glass, lace and linen. To watch the lace makers at work as well as to buy, try the Lace Centre at Balstraat, which is open on weekday afternoons from 2pm–6pm.

Bruges has no hypermarket. Two of the leading supermarkets are:

*Au Bon Marché,* Steenstraat
*Unic,* 548 Gistelstweg

### Markets

Burg, Wednesday and Saturday mornings
Markt, Saturday mornings
At Dijver, the flea market is open on Saturday and Sunday afternoons from 2pm, April–October.

### Parking

Banned in the Markt from 10pm Fri to 2pm Sat, and any cars already there will be towed away, even if they are owned by foreign tourists. Multi-storey car parks are available at the Zilverpand in Dweerstraat, and at the Biekorf in Naaldenstraat.

### Changing money

A bureau de change is available at the main Tourist Office at weekends when banks are closed. Banking hours are 9am–noon, 2pm–5pm, Mon–Fri but a few banks also open on Sat 9am–noon. The exchange rate in most hotels is not particularly favourable.

### Tourist Office

Markt 7, Tel (050) 33 07 11.
Open October–March: 9am–noon, 2pm–5.30pm weekdays; 9am–12.30pm, 2pm–5.30pm Sat; closed Sun and public holidays. April–September: 9am–7pm weekdays; 9am–12.30pm, 2pm–7pm weekends, and public holidays.
Stationstraat 27, Lissewege, Tel (050) 54 40 03. Mon–Fri: 9am–noon, 2pm–5.30pm, closed week-ends.

### Opening hours

Belfry (Markt), October–March: 10am–noon, 2pm–4pm weekdays and Sat; 10am–noon Sun and public holidays. April–September: 9.30–noon, 2pm–6pm daily.
Basilica of the Holy Blood (Burg), October–March: 10am–noon, 2pm–4pm.16. April–September: 9.30am–noon, 2pm–6pm. Closed Wed afternoons.
Town Hall (Burg), October–March: 10am–noon, 2pm–5pm. April–September: 9.30am–noon, 2pm to 6pm. Closed Tues.

Groeninge Museum (Dijver 12), October–March: 9.30am–noon, 2pm–5pm. April–September: 9.30am–6pm. Closed Tues.

Gruuthuse Museum (Dijver 12), October–March: 10am–noon, 2pm–5pm. April–September: 9am–12.30pm: 2pm–6pm. Closed Tues.

Combined tickets for these museums can be bought at each of them.

Church of Our Lady (Marian-straat): October–March: 10am–11.30am, 3pm–5pm, Mon–Sat. April–September: 10am–11.30am, 2.30pm–6pm Mon–Sat.

On Sundays and public holidays, the Burgundian mausoleums are open at the same times as the Church of our Lady is open on weekdays, but the church is open only in the afternoons.

Tours by horse-drawn cab from outside the Belfry.

Tours by boat from various points, 10am–6pm March–Nov.

## Accommodation

### Hotels

A reduction in Value Added Tax has helped to keep down the cost of staying in Bruges, but as a major tourist centre expect it to be both busy and expensive. Even with 51 hotels, advance booking is strongly advisable. In Belgium hotels are placed in five categories, from four stars to none, but those without stars are still clean and comfortable. The Tourist Office will advise on suitable hotels, make reservations for you, and even arrange baby-sitting!

*Holiday Inn*\*\*\*\* Boeveriestraat 2, Tel (050) 33 53 41. Even if you cannot afford to stay here, worth a visit to see how the facade of an old Capucine convent, removed during construction piece by piece, was then rebuilt to blend in with surrounding buildings. The original chapel has been restored at the rear of the hotel, making it possible to have wedding, reception and honeymoon all under one roof. The bar is furnished with old convent benches. All 128 rooms are air-conditioned, there is an indoor swimming pool and an outstanding restaurant. Not exactly the cheapest hotel in Bruges.

*Bourgeonsch Hof*\*\*\* Wollestraat 39, Tel (050) 33 16 45. Once a wealthy merchant's house, with a terrace overlooking the canal. Superb bedrooms, but only 12 of them.

*Duc de Bourgogne* Huidevettersplein 12, Tel (050) 33 20 38. One of the stops for the canal boats, a hotel with a marvellously picturesque setting and decor to match; the furnishings are 16th and 17th century. Superb French and Flemish cooking. Restaurant closed Sun eve and all Mon.

*Fevery* Collaert Mansionstraat 3, Tel (050) 33 12 69. Continental breakfast only, but quiet, and close to main shops. All 10 rooms with bath.

*Jacobs* Baliestraat 1, Tel (050) 33 98 32 or 33 98 31. Very friendly, run by a family. Continental breakfast only.

*Navara* St Jacobsstraat 41, Tel (050) 34 05 61. Less than 150 yards from the Belfry, former home of the Prince of Navara. Continental breakfast only. Napoleon stayed here and has still to pay his bill.

### Restaurants

A word of warning. Leading restaurants in Bruges, as in other parts of Belgium, are extremely expensive. One meal, with a slight indulgence on wines, could well cost as much as some people plan to spend on their entire holiday. The best advice is to consult your hotel manager, especially if he offers bed and breakfast only, and is therefore not hoping that you will eat in his own restaurant.

*De Snippe* Ezelstraat 52, Tel (050) 33 70 70. Tiny, unpretentions and packed. Booking vital. Food superb but certainly not a snip. . . .

*Civière d'Or* Markt 33, Tel (050) 33 17 93. In the old Fishmonger's Hall, popular with tourists, but quite expensive.

*Central* Markt 30, Tel (050) 33 18 05. Good food, reasonable prices.

*Saint-Joris* Markt 29, Tel (050) 33 60 62. Simple cooking, fast service, good value.

*Panier D'Or* Markt 28, Tel (050) 33 39 85. In the old Roofmakers' Hall, restaurant with famous history; 12 rooms.

## Damme

Damme is too close to Bruges to be considered separately. Once the port of Bruges, it lies along a canal route with beautiful views, and can be reached by boat during the summer months. Damme could once accommodate up to 100 ships at a time, but has long ceased to be of any importance as a harbour. Its narrow streets and passages are remarkably well preserved. A statue to Jacob van Maerlant, father of Dutch poets, stands in the market square.

Tourist Office: Jacob van Maerlantstraat 3, Tel (050) 35 33 19, October–March: open weekdays, April–September: open daily.

Opening hours: Town Hall (Markt), May–September 10 am–noon, 2pm–6pm. Closed rest of year.

Jacob van Maerlant Museum (Markt): October–April: 2pm–pm, daily. May–September: 10am–noon, 2pm–6pm, daily. Charles the Bold and Margaret of York, sister of Edward IV, were married in this house in July 1468.

Maritime Museum (Vaart Zuid 15), March–November: 9am–noon, 2pm–6pm. Closed the rest of the year.

Boat trips from Bruges: April–September, 5 trips each day, Napoleon canal Bruges to Damme Tel (050) 32 02 86.

Hotels: *De Gulden Kogge* Damsevaart–Zuid 12, Tel (050) 35 42 17. Six rooms.

*Clio*\*\* Gentsesteenweg 86, Sijsele, Tel (050) 35 39 42. Sixteen rooms.

Restaurant: *Den Heerd* Jacob van Maerlantstraat 7, Tel (050) 35 44 00.

# Train that car

## The easy way to cross Europe by car

*The motorail way*

Dover docks to Alexandria in Egypt without putting five miles on the clock seems a tall order. But it is possible to get to the Pyramids by car without driving across Europe, through Turkey, Lebanon and the Sinai Desert, precarious enough when you had only the climate to contend with, let alone the violent politics of the Near East.

For the sceptics, this is the route. First, car ferry by Townsend, Dover to Boulogne. Next, motorail Boulogne to Milan. Arrive at 6.30 am, leave the car at the station, spend the day in Milan. At 10 pm leave by motorail for Brindisi. The following day, take the car ferry from Brindisi to Corfu, run by the Adriatic Line. The next morning take the Sol Maritime Services' ship arriving from Venice on to the port of Athens, Piraeus; then to Heraklion in Crete; and finally, on the same ship, from Heraklion to Alexandria.

Not everyone, of course, wants to spend a week crossing Western Europe and the Mediterranean with their car, but it does illustrate the extraordinary range of services available. Equally feasible if you wish to avoid driving as much as possible are the following:

Motorail Boulogne to Biarritz, drive across border to San Sebastian; motorail San Sebastian to Madrid, Madrid to Alicante; ferry from Alicante to the Canary Islands. Or motorail Paris to Madrid, then by changing stations, Madrid to Algeciras; Algeciras to Tangier by ferry.

Instead, Boulogne to Milan; then, by

changing stations, Milan to Villa San Giovanni in the toe of Italy; ferry from Reggio di Calabria to Palermo in Sicily and on to Syracuse, then ferry to Valetta in Malta. Or, motorail Brussels to Ljubljana in Yugoslavia; Ljubljana to Belgrade; Belgrade to Sarajevo.

All heady stuff, but logistically quite possible, and not solely for millionaires considering how cheap train travel is in Italy and Spain and sea travel is in the Eastern Mediterranean.

Indeed motorail may actually cost very little more than driving. Many motorists never properly calculate the cost of driving long distances, which may include:

Motorway tolls
Overnight accommodation
Additional meals
Petrol and oil
Wear and tear on the car (especially tyres) and even
On-the-spot fines (if you are unlucky)

Not to mention wear and tear on the driver and the passengers.

Even without the intangible elements of wear and tear, for two people travelling at the height of the season in a sizeable car, say an estate, motorail from Boulogne to Avignon with couchettes could actually cost them only a few pounds more per person than driving. This is because French Motorail offers a substantial discount on Sealink ferries and a fixed rate for the complete journey. So any motorist with inflexible holiday arrangements forcing him to travel on, say, a Saturday morning in August, would make a considerable saving.

Direct services from the Channel ports, and from Lille, Paris and Brussels, are remarkably extensive (see map pp. 120–1). They include the following:

| | |
|---|---|
| Calais to Narbonne | Seasonal |
| Calais to Nice | Daily |
| Boulogne to Avignon | Seasonal |
| Boulogne to Biarritz | Seasonal |
| Boulogne to Milan | Seasonal |
| Boulogne to Narbonne | Seasonal |
| Boulogne to Brive | Seasonal |
| Boulogne to Bordeaux | Seasonal |
| Boulogne to Frejus | Seasonal |
| Lille to Nice | Daily |
| Paris to Nice | Daily |
| Paris to Briançon | Seasonal (winter) |
| Paris to Milan | Seasonal |
| Paris to Madrid | Daily |
| Paris to Lisbon | Winter, weekly; Summer, daily |
| Brussels to Milan | Seasonal |
| Brussels to Ljubljana | Seasonal |

Although all the stations offering, or specialising in, motorail services are sign-posted close by as 'trains auto couchettes' (T.A.C.) or occasionally as 'car-sleeper', some are not particularly easy to find.

### Calais
Hoverport cars for the motorail terminal at the Gare Maritime must take the route back towards Calais town centre as far as the main ferry terminal, from where the motorail embarkation point, a right turn out of the ferry terminal is clearly marked. The ferry terminal is for Sealink sailings to and from Dover Eastern Docks and for Townsend Thoresen. However motorists using a Sealink sailing to Dover Western Docks have a separate embarkation point much closer to the terminal.

### Boulogne
Follow the road out of the car ferry terminal, keeping right with the railway line on your left, until you reach a 'T' junction at the end of the rue de Solferino. Turn right into rue St Vincent de Paul, which leads into rue Alexandre Adam and the motorail terminal. From the hoverport, follow the normal route to the motorway as far as the Viaduc Jean Jaurès, which passes over the rail spur to the motorail terminal. Filter right down from the Viaduct, turn left and under it, left again into the rue Solferino and follow the car ferry route. Shorter routes to the motorail terminal exist, but are more open to error.

### Lille
The motorail service is from Gare Centrale (and not Gare Lille Sud, which can be glimpsed from the Dunkerque motorway).

Remain on the motorway until you see signs for the centre of town, follow them to Place Général de Gaulle, and the station is close by. Facing the entrance in the Place de la Gare, the embarkation point for cars is to the right, on rue de Tournai.

## Brussels

Four stations are used by main line services in Brussels, but motorail operates only from Schaerbeek. From Bruges, drive into the centre of Brussels passing first the Gare du Nord on your left, then the botanic gardens. Just after the road bears sharp right, swing left into Chausseé de Louvain, them, at the next main junction, a further left into Boulevard Général Wahis, which leads into Boulevard Lambermunt. The Gare de Schaerbeek is off to the right.

## Paris

Many motorail services use the purpose-built terminal at Bercy, which can be reached from the Channel ports using the A3 motorway on to the boulevard périphérique (see map p. 139) and then leaving at the Porte de Bercy. The slip road exit, rue Robert Etlin, leads into the quai de Bercy, at which point you should have the River Seine on your left. At the Pont de Bercy, turn right into the Boulevard de Bercy, and the entrance to the Gare de Paris-Bercy (T.A.C.) is on the right at the corner of rue Corbineau.

Outward and homeward motorail journeys may start and finish at different stations. Other motorail termini used on the popular routes south include Charolais reached from the périphérique via the Porte de Bercy (again), the quai de Bercy, the Boulevard de Bercy and then by a left turn into the rue de Charolais; the station is on your left. For Tolbiac, the T.A.C. station for the Gare d'Austerlitz, leave the périphérique at the junction Porte d'Ivry, proceed along the quai de la Gare with the Seine on your right. The station entrance is on your left just after the Pont de Tolbiac.

## Booking

Although some travel agents will handle motorail bookings, not all of them do, and it may prove more efficient to book with the specialist organisations concerned. In the case of services from Brussels, through the Motorail Reservation Office at Victoria Station, London; for services starting within France, from French Railways in Piccadilly. The French reservation system is computerised, but bookings are not

*Loading a car on to the wagon*

PRINCIPAL MOTORAIL ROUTES

accepted on the computer until three months before the departure date. As many passengers wish to be certain of their travel arrangements earlier than that, French Railways hold earlier reservations in a strict order of booking, and program the computer on the first available day for a particular reservation.

Mistakes are extremely rare, but it is nevertheless a wise precaution to check your tickets before departure. Apart from the train tickets themselves, you should be in possession of a separate ticket for the car in each direction and for any sleeping accommodation. On most trains, you will have a choice between couchettes, which are simply bunks with no washing facilities, and T2 or T3 sleepers, which are purpose-built compartments with either two or three beds inside, and private washing facilities. Check that your ticket is for the correct type of accommodation and that your sleeping berths are all in the same compartment (if they should be).

### Loading

When loading your car in England, if you are carrying a roof rack, remember that everything on it will have to be removed at the motorail embarkation point and stored within the car. French Railways have a fat file on items that motorists have brought on their roof rack and which, to their dismay, could never be squeezed into the car itself.

At the embarkation point an official will mark on your ticket any dents or scratches already visible on your car, to prevent some unscrupulous motorist from claiming that they occurred during the journey, as your car is insured by French Railways against damage. In the million-to-one chance of your windscreen being broken, that would be replaced, too. Do not expect your car to travel through the night without gathering a good deal of dirt from passing trains, but nowhere near as much as it would have done making the same journey by road.

In Paris and Boulogne, your car will probably be driven on to the purpose-built wagons by officials; elsewhere, you may be invited to drive it on yourself, though you do not have to if you feel happier leaving it to the railway staff. Your car will be locked and sealed for the journey, and that may be the last glimpse you will get of it until you arrive at your destination the following morning.

Even if you have a sleeping compartment for your party, keep the luggage you take on the train to a minimum. Sleeping compartments are cleverly designed but, apart from first class, not really spacious.

Every sleeping car is manned by an attendant, who may well speak English; he will show you to your compartment, take away your tickets and (if you are crossing a frontier) your passports for official checks later; provide cold meals and drinks, and, unless your train arrives very early in the morning, a free breakfast with tea, coffee or hot chocolate. Many passengers like to bring their own food on board after a quick dash to a Continental supermarket, which is obviously less expensive. Although restaurant meals are available on a few international routes, it is wise not to depend on them.

In the morning your tickets and passports will be returned to you by your attendant (nocturnal visits by emigration and customs officials being almost unheard of), along with a bill for any food and drink, other than breakfast, that you have ordered from him during the journey. On some routes your breakfast vouchers may need to be presented at the station buffet to obtain breakfast on arrival, but this does not waste any time in practice, because it will take a few minutes for all the cars to be unloaded. Do check your vehicle for any possible damage, as it will be too late to make a claim later.

On a very few services, cars arrive later by a separate train; as this involves more delay, these are best avoided – with one exception. From Paris it is possible to book your car on the Paris-Lyon/Avignon/Marseille motorail service, and to travel separately from the Gare de Lyon on the Train à Grand Vitesse, the T.G.V. A marvellous, unforgettable way to start – or end – your holiday.

# South to the sun

## The motorways of Europe and recommended routes to holiday destinations

In many ways motorways have opened up a new era for the independent traveller, making round trips possible in a fortnight which 100 years ago would have taken several months, but they do have disadvantages. In many countries the cost of using motorways is high – for example, tolls for a medium-sized car travelling from Calais to Nice will amount to about £26. They are no way to acquire a feel of the country through which you are travelling, and although motorway meals are a good deal more sophisticated on the Continent than they are in most UK service areas, they are no substitute for eating in relaxed surroundings elsewhere. The sustained high speeds of motorway driving may place too great a strain on both the driver and his vehicle. Breakdowns or traffic jams or indeed any problem arising on an autoroute may leave you in a concrete strait-jacket from which there is no easy escape.

### Joining the motorway network

For all that, on balance, you are probably going to join the motorway as soon as possible. In France, two of the principal ports of entry from Dover, Calais and Boulogne, both offer easy access to the motorway that leads to Paris, the A26 (see maps p. 125).

Leaving Calais: whether or not you have decided to venture into the town centre, to save time on quiet days or to do some shopping, you will be looking, initially, for the N43 (which stands for Route Nationale 43) to St-Omer. You will be quite certain when you have found the correct road because it is liberally signposted with indications that the A26 is up ahead, and that it is *à Péage*, or toll, motorway. In all you have 12 miles non-motorway driving, through Ardres to the present starting-point for the motorway at Nordausques.

Leaving Boulogne: the route to the A26 still has some pitfalls for the unwary, despite considerable improvements in signposting. For example, should you decide to go into the principal shopping area of Boulogne, some of the signs for 'Paris' will lead you to the N1, the old non-motorway road, and not towards the A26. There is also a difference between the lorry route to the motorway, which is shown by a lorry symbol on the blue and white autoroute sign, and the motorist's route to the A26, which is usually indicated by a car symbol on the same basic sign. The route to the motorway is on the N42, also signposted 'St-Omer', through Colembert and Lumbres, with A26 *'péage'* signs appearing at intervals. After 27 miles, the A26 signs will be marked 'Reims, Paris' and indicate a left turn on to the motorway.

Leaving Dunkerque: simplicity itself. The actual port is well to the west of Dunkerque, in the Calais direction, so there is no need to enter Dunkerque at all. Just outside the port, join the N1 for direct access to the A25 autoroute, following signs to 'Lille' for 12 miles. Outside Lille, there is a choice of motorway routes through Belgium or south through Paris.

Leaving Ostende: Outside the ferry port prepare yourself for one fairly sharp left turn, but thereafter the route is quite straightforward, joining the A10 signposted 'Brugge' (Bruges) and 'Bruxelles', merging shortly with the motorway.

Leaving Zeebrugge: Outside the ferry port, the N298, which is clearly signposted, leads to Bruges; the N298 also skirts the city to the east, enabling motorists intending to travel on to Brussels by way of the motorway to do so without any delay.

**Tolls**
In Belgium and West Germany, motorways follow the British practice of not levying tolls on motorists. In France, Italy and Spain, with one or two exceptions, which include stretches of motorway within major conurbations, motorists are expected to pay. Switzerland has an annual tax (see p. 132). Some examples of tolls are given on p. 134. The system is actually quite simple. At most toll booths at the entrance to a motorway, you collect a computerised card, occasionally from the toll keeper, but usually from an automatic dispenser by pressing a button. When you leave the motorway, or when you come to a toll collecting point or *péage*, you hand over the ticket and pay the appropriate charge. At many booths this will be displayed on an automatic sign, so you don't have to understand French, Italian or Spanish. All the charges are based on a combination of the cubic capacity of your vehicle and the number of miles covered, but working out what you will pay from the cards is sometimes quite difficult. If you have a particularly obscure make of car, the toll keeper may overestimate its cubic capacity: by all means point this out, but if he will not budge, simply insist on a receipt and complain to the operating company after the holiday.

Occasionally, payment is made instead in advance, sometimes, if you have change, by throwing the correct coins into an automatic device to raise the barrier. If you do not have sufficient money in the local currency, virtually all the toll points will accept payment in the currency of a neighbouring country or in sterling. However, their exchange rate may not be as good as at a bank; they not always accept small coins; and they may give you change in the local currency, and in coins, which if you are leaving the country may not be of much use subsequently. In Italy, too, because of a shortage of coins, you may be given change in vouchers which can only be used in Italy, or in telephone tokens, or postage stamps, or even sweets. At some toll booths, travellers' cheques are also accepted.

*Opposite: Joining the motorway network from the Channel ports*

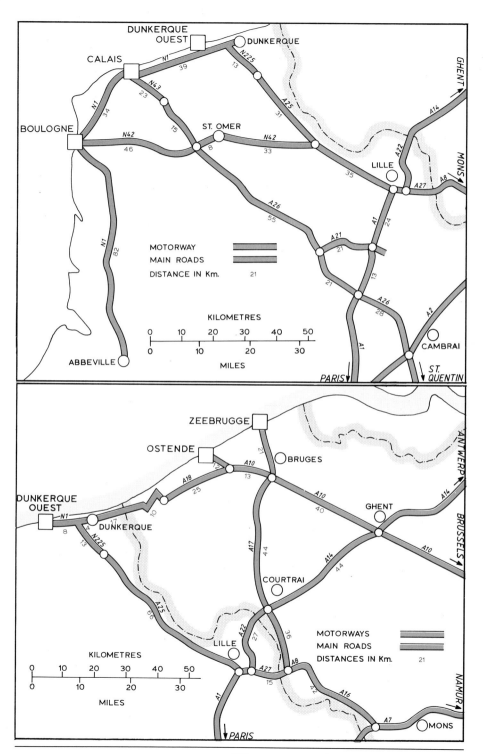

## Petrol coupons

In Italy, prepaid petrol coupons, bought in advance from a motoring organisation in this country or from the Automobile Club Italia (A.C.I.) offices on the Italian border, include as a bonus five free motorway toll vouchers valid for northern Italy, and eight additional vouchers if you purchase the 'Italia Sud' package. The petrol coupons are supplied in litres rather than lire, so the price you pay fluctuates according to the exchange rate. To obtain the coupons in this country, applicants must make a personal visit to their motoring organisation office, complete an application form, and present both their passport and the registration document of the car to be used in Italy. They will receive a Carta Carburante Turistica (Tourist Fuel Card) which should be kept with the coupons for possible inspection at a service station, though Italian garages rarely bother with it.

Unused coupons should be surrendered at any A.C.I. office at the frontier, whereupon their value will be refunded in local currency, or it is possible to obtain a refund through the issuing office in the UK.

Coupons to cut the cost of petrol are also available for Yugoslavia, obtainable at the frontier. Yugoslavia is already among the cheapest for petrol on the Continent, so with a further discount by way of coupons, their petrol is very cheap indeed. Elsewhere the differences are no longer substantial, so few people bother nowadays to take a spare can of petrol with them. It is against the law in any case to carry petrol in a can in Italy, Greece and Portugal, and it is banned on ferries and on Continental motorail. The space is much better used for a can of engine oil, which is much more expensive than in the UK, and often available only in large containers – making the purchase still more painful.

However, real savings can be made in fuel consumption. The prudent family thinks twice before putting a roof rack on the car, which adds enormously to wind resistance and in consequence to fuel consumption. If you really cannot reduce the amount of luggage, and it simply will

*Take a toll card as you join the motorway*

not go in the boot and the car, attaching a small trailer to the back may be a better solution – though it could increase charges on some ferry routes out of Dover. Both a heavy load and fierce acceleration can also increase consumption. The key to economic driving is gradual acceleration and the use of the highest possible gear that enables the car to pull smoothly. On a long motorway journey, the overall saving can be astonishingly high.

## Service Stations

Food at service stations on the motorway is generally more expensive than in the UK, but also markedly superior. The Pavesi restaurants in Italy, for example, are particularly good.

## Regulations

In most countries the motorway regulations are similar to those in UK. The outside lane, be it the second or third, is intended only for overtaking. The hard shoulder is for emergency stops only, and stopping without some physically identifiable reason can result in a fine on the spot.

For example, cleaning mud off the headlights could be considered a reasonable excuse for stopping; a stop to change drivers, or because the driver felt tired, would not be. In such circumstances, he would be expected to continue to the next exit and leave the motorway, or go into a suitable service or rest area.

**Breakdowns**

A breakdown is, of course, always a good reason to stop on the hard shoulder. On the Continent, you should position your warning triangle, put on your hazard lights*, and walk to the nearest emergency telephone – they are two kilometres apart. In France, you will be connected to the police, who will send out a breakdown vehicle from a nearby garage. If a repair in under 30 minutes is feasible, they must complete it on the spot, and at a prescribed motorway rate. Otherwise, they will tow you to a garage of your choice.

In West Germany, it is the highway station rather than the police who respond to routine emergency calls. They work in close co-operation with motorway filling stations, which, unlike those in the UK, in many cases can offer their own breakdown service, either on the spot on the motorway, or back in the service area.

In Italy, the A.C.I. operates a motorway breakdown service, using its own staff, and available to any visiting motorist. Those carrying a Tourist Fuel Card can obtain the service without charge.

In Spain, the breakdown service is usually provided by the authority operating the motorway. There is, however, a perverse demarcation line between what they are prepared to do at an official rate, and the service the motorist requires. If your car needs to be towed, the motorway authority will indeed tow it, but only to the nearest exit ramp on the motorway, from where they will summon a local garage to complete both the tow and the repair.

In Belgium, the Touring Club Royal de Belgique (TCB), and the Royal Automobile Club de Belgique (RACB) each

*except in Austria, where the use of hazard lights is restricted to accidents only.

operate a motorway breakdown service.

Some breakdowns occur because a car has not been properly serviced before setting out, or because the vehicle is overloaded and driven at too demanding a pace. For all that, breakdowns in summer are statistically rare in proportion to the number of vehicles on the road. It is in winter that far more breakdowns are experienced, and the great majority of them are unnecessary.

The most common explanation of stranded vehicles in winter is ignition failure. This, in turn, is often due to poor insulation, wet leads, a poorly-charged battery and damp or defective spark plugs. Regular attention given to the battery, the distributor points and the spark plugs will eliminate most causes of ignition failure.

Driving in adverse weather requires a substantial adjustment in technique. Only gentle pressure on the brakes will avoid locking the wheels on a really slippery surface, so the effective stopping distance will be far, far greater. Facing a hill in icy conditions, select the gear and the moment to move so that you can be sure of reaching the top without hesitation. On wet roads, be comforted by the swishing sound of the tyres moving over water; a change in sound may well indicate black ice. On foggy roads, drive with the side window down, to hear unseen dangers more quickly.

Equip your car for the worst. Keep, in the back not the boot, waterproof clothing and boots. Keep, in the glove compartment, a de-icer spray and an ice scraper. Keep, in the boot, a spade, a flashing torch, and a tow rope.

Yet the worst will probably not happen. On the Continent, prodigious efforts are made to keep open the main motorway routes because they are the lifeblood of international trade. Even in the worst conditions, major roads are rarely closed for more than a few hours. And really bad weather is rare: for the greater part of the winter a motorist can drive on the Continent, even to skiing resorts, knowing that his journey will be almost as fast and a good deal less crowded than in the summer.

**Toll motorways**
**Non-toll motorways**
**Motorways under construction**
**Main roads**

Kilometres
0   50   100   150   200

# MAJOR MOTORWAYS OF EUROPE

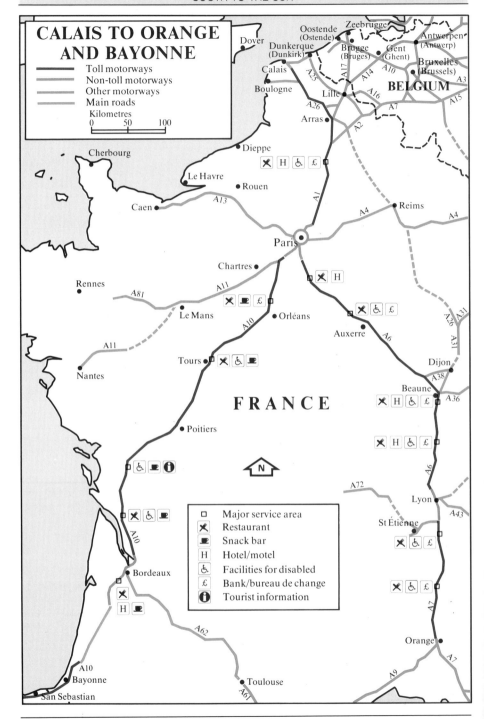

**CALAIS TO ORANGE AND BAYONNE**

Toll motorways
Non-toll motorways
Other motorways
Main roads

Kilometres
0    50    100

| □ | Major service area |
| ✕ | Restaurant |
| 🍴 | Snack bar |
| H | Hotel/motel |
| ♿ | Facilities for disabled |
| £ | Bank/bureau de change |
| ❶ | Tourist information |

FRANCE

BELGIUM

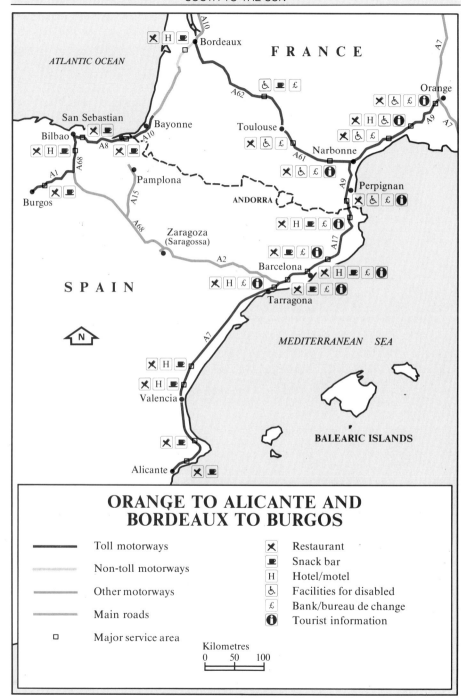

# ORANGE TO ALICANTE AND BORDEAUX TO BURGOS

| | |
|---|---|
| ──────── Toll motorways | ✕ Restaurant |
| ···················· Non-toll motorways | 🍴 Snack bar |
| ──────── Other motorways | H Hotel/motel |
| ──────── Main roads | ♿ Facilities for disabled |
| □ Major service area | £ Bank/bureau de change |
| | ℹ Tourist information |

Kilometres
0    50    100

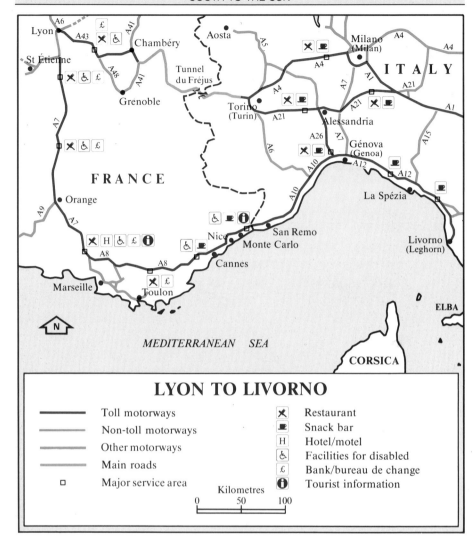

## LYON TO LIVORNO

| | | | |
|---|---|---|---|
| ▬▬▬ | Toll motorways | ✗ | Restaurant |
| ▬▬▬ | Non-toll motorways | ▣ | Snack bar |
| ▬▬▬ | Other motorways | H | Hotel/motel |
| ▬▬▬ | Main roads | ♿ | Facilities for disabled |
| ▫ | Major service area | £ | Bank/bureau de change |
| | | ❶ | Tourist information |

Kilometres
0   50   100

**Swiss motorway tax**

All cars and motorcycles using motorways in Switzerland must pay a tax of 30 Sw Frs (about £10). Payment may be made at any Swiss Customs Frontier post or to the Swiss National Tourist Office, the RAC or the AA in this country. A windscreen disc, acknowledging payment of the tax, has to be displayed on the front windscreen of the car and is not transferable from one vehicle to another. A caravan or trailer is also liable for a 30 Sw Frs tax.

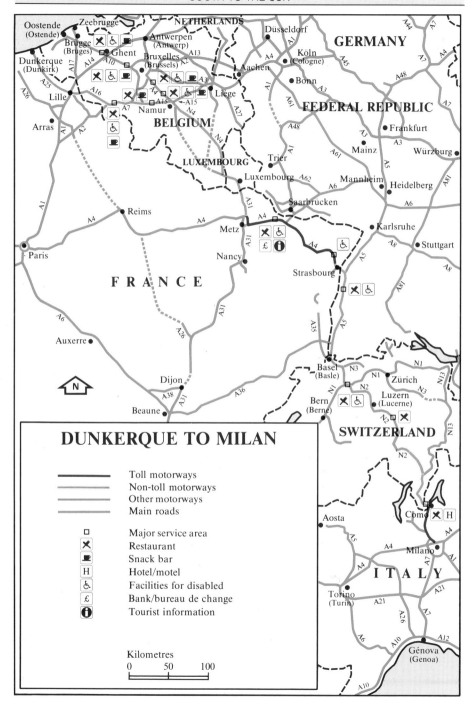

## DUNKERQUE TO MILAN

| | |
|---|---|
| ────── | Toll motorways |
| ────── | Non-toll motorways |
| ────── | Other motorways |
| ────── | Main roads |
| □ | Major service area |
| ✕ | Restaurant |
| ☕ | Snack bar |
| H | Hotel/motel |
| ♿ | Facilities for disabled |
| £ | Bank/bureau de change |
| ❶ | Tourist information |

Kilometres
0    50    100

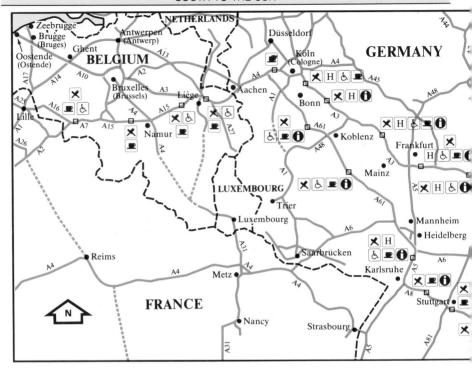

## Speed limits for cars in Western Europe

| | built-up areas kmh | outside built-up areas kmh | motorways kmh |
|---|---|---|---|
| Austria | 50 | 100 | 130 |
| Belgium | 60 | 90/120 | 120 |
| Denmark | 60 | 80 | 100 |
| France† | 60 | 90/110 | 100 non-toll 130 toll |
| West Germany | 50 | 100/130 | 130* |
| Greece | 50 | 80 | 100 |
| Holland | 50 | 80 | 100 |
| Italy | 50 | 80/100** | 90/140** |
| Luxembourg | 60 | 90 | 120 |
| Portugal | 60 | 90 | 120 |
| Spain | 60 | 90/100 | 120 |
| Switzerland | 60 | 80 | 120 |
| Yugoslavia | 60 | 80/100 | 120 |

†limits reduced in poor weather
*recommended
**according to cylinder capacity

### Seat belts

It is a general rule that drivers and front-seat passengers must wear seat belts· if fitted. This rule holds throughout Europe except for Italy (where they are strongly recommended) and in built-up areas in Portugal and Spain. Visitors to Austria and West Germany should now remember that rear-seat passengers are also required to wear seat belts if the car is fitted with them. On-the-spot fines may be imposed if motorists ignore these regulations.

### Tolls

Some examples of motorway tolls
**France**
Paris–Bordeaux: approx 160 francs
Paris–Le Perthus: 230 francs
Paris–Cannes: 200 francs
**Spain**
La Junquera–Alicante: 3660 pesetas
**Italy**
Milan–Rome: according to car length
16,800–36,950 lire

# OSTENDE TO VENICE, VIENNA AND SALZBURG

| | |
|---|---|
| ━━━ Toll motorways | ✖ Restaurant |
| ━━━ Non-toll motorways | ☕ Snack bar |
| ━━━ Main roads | H Hotel/motel |
| ━━━ Other motorways | ♿ Facilities for disabled |
| ▫ Major service area | £ Bank/bureau de change |
| | ❶ Tourist information |

Kilometres
0    50    100

GERMANY
(D.D.R.)

CZECHOSLOVAKIA

rzburg

Nürnberg
(Nuremberg)

Regensburg

Passau

Wien
(Vienna)

FEDERAL REPUBLIC

Linz

München
(Munich)

Salzburg

AUSTRIA

Graz

Innsbruck

Brenner Pass

Klagenfurt

Maribor

SWITZ.

Cortina
d'Ampezzo

Udine

Ljubljana

Zagreb

Trento

ITALY

YUGOSLAVIA

Lago
di Garda

Trieste

Rijeka

Verona

Padova
(Padua)

Venezia
(Venice)

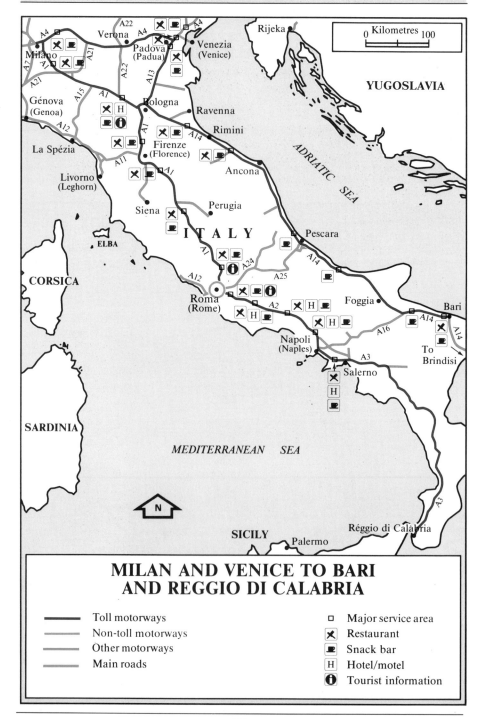

## MILAN AND VENICE TO BARI
## AND REGGIO DI CALABRIA

| | Toll motorways | | ▫ | Major service area |
| | Non-toll motorways | | ✖ | Restaurant |
| | Other motorways | | ▣ | Snack bar |
| | Main roads | | H | Hotel/motel |
| | | | ❶ | Tourist information |

# Paris – a diversion

Paris poses a dilemma for British motorists. Even if they have visited the city before, the temptation to do so again is almost irresistible, when the chances are that it lies directly on their routes to the holiday areas of the south of France, Spain, or Italy. However they know to their cost that spending even a day in Paris while in possession of a motor car can be little short of disaster. So if you are determined to sample Paris on your way south, or on your way home, first find your parking place.

Many people suppose that the ring road, the boulevard périphérique, is routed a long way from the most attractive and popular parts of Paris; in fact it runs within four blocks of the Arc de Triomphe. The exit which makes sampling Paris comparatively easy is Porte Maillot, on the western side of Paris. To reach it from the south, take the A6A on to the périphérique and go westwards; to reach it from the north, take the A1 almost to Porte de la Chapelle, then take a right filter on to the périphérique going west ('ouest') and leave again at Porte Maillot, filtering right and passing under the boulevard. Porte Maillot itself is a huge, circular boulevard, with traffic running anti-clockwise. It has two car parks, one on the south side to which you come first, and one to the north side, immediately in front of the Palais des Congrès. If these should be full, two further car parks are available close by: one to the north, on the road that runs to the right of the Palais des Congrès, just past the Palais, on the right-hand side; one to the south, down avenue de Malakoff,

*Place de la Concorde and the Eiffel Tower*

137

across the busy avenue Foch, at the start of a one-way street, the rue de la Pompe.

You would have to be very unlucky indeed not to find a single space in one of these four car parks, and having deposited your vehicle, the Arc de Triomphe is only two stops away on the Paris underground, the Métro, from the Porte Maillot station.

### The Métro

The Métro remains the quickest and easiest way of visiting different parts of Paris, and travel on it is relatively cheap because Parisian transport receives a large subsidy, funded partly by central government and partly by local businesses. Each ticket is valid for a complete journey, however long, and they are discounted if you buy them in groups of ten – ask for *un carnet*. If you intend to use the Métro frequently, and are staying in Paris overnight, tourist tickets are also available. These have the advantage of offering first-class Métro travel, which is much more comfortable during the rush hours.

All the Métro signs are based on the terminus of the particular line on which you elect to travel – for example, from Maillot to get to the nearest Métro to the Arc de Triomphe, which is Étoile, follow the signs marked 'direction Château de Vincennes', Château de Vincennes being the eastern end of the line which, two stops from Maillot, reaches Étoile.

Métro tickets are also valid on buses and you can get back on a bus on the same route without paying again as long as you are within two fare stages. Bus routes are clearly marked at most bus stops, and buses have the advantage of providing you with a view on the way to your destination, but they are just as vulnerable as ordinary cars in traffic jams, except on those few routes where a bus and taxi lane is rigidly enforced. A good pair of walking shoes is essential to see Paris – and, for that matter, to cope with the Métro, whose interchanges can be so far apart, up steps and down dingy passageways, that you may wonder if you are still in the same station.

### In central Paris

For the more adventurous, parking in the centre of Paris is still possible, but requires an element of luck. Empty meters are almost unheard of, and expensive to park

*Arc de Triomphe*

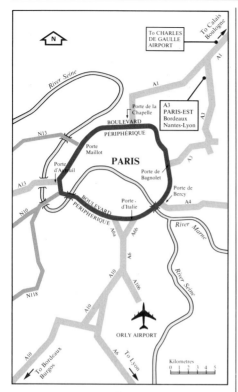

*Routes into and around Paris*

mous. It should also be noted that it is illegal to park any car in the same place on the streets, however otherwise legitimate, for more than 24 hours; and that there is an absolute ban on caravans in the centre of Paris.

However, it is possible to drive round Paris – magnificent after dark, when a great many public buildings are floodlit – and to park for almost nothing, with a little ingenuity. Many of the superior hotels have garages, and charge guests only a modest fee for parking. There are also unexpected little parks near some tourist attractions, where in theory you are expected to move the car when you leave, but in practice no one checks. For example, the Bateaux-Mouche company operates glass-topped boats on a river excursion between the Eiffel Tower and Notre Dame, virtually every day of the year, departing every 40 minutes during the summer peak. The boats leave from a pier near the Pont d'Alma, on the Right Bank (essentially the north side of the Seine), and there is a car park for patrons. Lunch and dinner are served on two special, slightly longer sailings, both surprisingly good meals considering that this is, unashamedly, an out-and-out tourist attraction.

**What to see**
On a first visit to Paris, it might be felt essential to see the avenue des Champs Élysées, the Place de la Concorde, which once contained the guillotine, the banks of the Seine, Notre Dame, the Latin quarter, and Montmartre. From the Métro station Abbesses, there is a funicular up to the Sacré Coeur basilica: the view from its steps over the Parisian skyline is arguably the best in the city. Unless you have a great deal of time to spare, settle for a sight of the Eiffel Tower from the bottom rather than the top, as the view is overrated except perhaps on a perfectly clear day, the charges exorbitant, and the queues formidable in summer.

If you are feeling in expansive mood, a cup of coffee or a glass of wine at the Café de la Paix is expensive but far better value

at; but in the 'blue' zone immediately outside the 'grey' meter zone, you can park for one hour at a time, provided that you display a parking disc inside the windscreen. These *disques de contrôle* take the form of a clock face and must be set to show the time of your arrival. You can get them from hotels, garages, police stations or many travel agencies. The only exception to the one hour limit during the day is the period 12.30 to 2.30 pm. Even for traffic wardens, a two-hour lunch stop is sacrosanct. There are no restrictions between 7pm and 9am.

Do not be tempted to ignore the parking regulations. Although parking tickets will probably not be pursued to the UK, cars, including those with foreign number plates, are towed away in great numbers. The expense in retrieving your car is considerable, and the inconvenience enor-

for money. If the tourists flock there, then so do the Parisians, because it remains a marvellous place to sit and watch the world go by, to see and be seen.

Café de la Paix is in Place d'Opéra (Métro station Opéra), which is only a brief walk past the Paris Opera House, to the Boulevard Haussmann. Here are two of the most famous department stores in the world, Au Printemps and Galeries Lafayette, where practically everything worth buying in France is on display . . . except food. A left turn back towards Place de la Concorde takes you into rue Tronchet and then into Place de la Madeleine, where you will find Fauchon, the greatest food shop anywhere. Go early in the morning if you can, before the tremendous displays disappear piecemeal into buyers' shopping bags.

### Where to eat

Eating at a restaurant in Paris remains something of a lottery. With more than 7,500 restaurants, it would take you ten years, lunchtime and dinner, to sample them all, by which time perhaps 1,000 would have changed hands, or, more important, changed chefs. If you are pressed for time, you may have to settle for an unpretentious looking restaurant in the Latin quarter, whose main customers are impecunious but nevertheless fastidious students.

One golden rule. Never eat at a night spot. It will always be over-priced and nearly always indifferently cooked. The Moulin Rouge, in Montmartre, and the Lido, on the Champs Élysées, remain the best shows, with a fixed price for a seat at a table including a mediocre bottle of champagne between two. As both offer substantial commissions to hotels and agencies to steer business their way, visting them in person early during the day, and trying for a discount for cash, has been known to be successful.

### Bargains

Bargains are, however, few and far between in Paris. The flea market at St Ouen, on the périphérique, rarely has any.

The cheapest place to shop conveniently is the Prisunic on, improbable though it may seem, the Champs Élysées. Museums are free on Sundays, but predictably it is then that they are the most crowded. The left luggage office at the Louvre Museum is free every day, but the Louvre itself is a daunting prospect that requires a week to do it justice, unless all you want is a quick glimpse of the Mona Lisa. Wine in Paris can be a bargain if bought direct from the wine merchants of the Porte de Bercy, on the right bank of the Seine. The VAT you pay will be refunded – eventually – in the United Kingdom, but only if you have a passion for paperwork.

### Going round Paris

If neither your money or your time allows a visit to Paris, circumnavigating the city is now a lot easier than it used to be. The French have built a relief road which enables the tourist to use a much shorter distance of the périphérique than when it was first opened in 1973. Going south, this road is a turning off the A1, the main autoroute into Paris, shortly after passing Charles de Gaulle airport on your left. The signpost reads:

A3
Paris Est
Bordeaux
Nantes-Lyon

and will be a right-hand filter even though, of course, the A3 will thereafter take you off to your left, skirting Paris to the east. It does not join the périphérique until the entry point known as Porte de Bagnolet. Then, at Porte d'Italie, prepare to join the A6B autoroute by moving into the right-hand lane. A trap for the unwary is an exit marked N7, which was of course, the old pre-autoroute, way to the south. Ignore that and take, 100 yards on, the next exit which is for the A6B. At this point alongside will be a separate but parallel motorway, the A6A, which merges with the A6B to become the simply the A6. Follow signs for 'Lyon' throughout.

Going north, the shortest and usually

*Cathedral of Notre Dame and a bateau-mouche*

the quickest route to the Channel ports will again be by way of the A6B, joining the périphérique at the Porte d'Italie and going east (or as the French say, 'est') until just short of the Porte de Bagnolet the autoroute A3 is signposted 'Lille, Bruxelles'. The A3 autoroute takes you northeast to merge with the A1, the Autoroute du Nord, for the Channel ports. However, if you find it impossible to avoid the rush hour afternoon peak, or one of the weekend days when traffic is at its height, experience shows that the western route around Paris, though substantially further, can sometimes offer a much clearer run. Join the périphérique going west (or 'ouest') by taking the A6A instead of the A6B continue on the périphérique until

the exit known as Porte de la Chapelle, then take the A1, the Autoroute du Nord, following signs to Charles de Gaulle and 'Lille'.

Any advice depends on roadworks in existence at the time of travel, and as these roads carry so much traffic, frequent repairs are necessary. The Continental Traffic Report on BBC Radio Two each weekend, and in summer The Travel Show on Wednesday evenings on BBC2 carry regular reports on the situation around Paris. In some circumstances it can be advisable to avoid the A3 altogether, or one particular section of the périphérique, so obtaining the latest information just before you travel can make all the difference to your journey.

# Help!

## What to do when something goes wrong

A problem shared may not be exactly a problem halved, but a problem covered by insurance is certainly more bearable, if no less disagreeable. The most extensive cover you can afford to take out for yourself, your party and your car is beyond doubt a worthwhile investment.

Even if you have arranged a Green Card before you depart for the Continent, and you have fully comprehensive insurance on your vehicle, there are many misadventures that will fall outside the policy. In particular, should your car break down or be involved in an accident on the Continent, not only would you be deprived of transport when you needed it the most, but if the defect or damage proved serious, it might need to be taken back to the UK on a transporter or railway wagon – an incredibly expensive exercise that could prove financially disastrous.

### RAC Travellers Bond

What is quite essential, then, must be some kind of vehicle recovery insurance, such as the RAC Travellers Bond, available to members and non-members alike. There are several policies on the market but the RAC scheme is particularly advantageous for owners with cars registered more than ten years ago, which of course are more vulnerable under the pressure of a high-speed Continental run. Most policies include roadside assistance; reimbursement of the costs of a tow into a garage should you need one; garage storage and labour charges; the cost of air freighting spare parts; a hire car while your own car is off the road; recovery of the car and repatriation of your entire party if the worst comes the worst and it cannot be repaired before the end of your holiday. The RAC is particularly well equipped to deal with breakdowns in the area where they seem to occur most frequently, on the final run to the Channel ports. Two rescue vehicles are stationed at Calais, and in the summer months there is a special RAC office open between Thursday and Saturday at St Omer.

## Car accidents

Many breakdowns, of course, are the result of damage to a car in an accident. Again, the most likely place for an accident seems to be close to the Channel ports, where motorists, perhaps unfamiliar with driving on the right, are hurrying towards their holiday resort, or rushing back at the last minute to catch a ferry.

A set procedure should always be followed in the event of an accident. Taking care of anyone injured should always be a priority, by summoning an ambulance and by moving anyone actually lying in the path of oncoming traffic. Send someone away from the scene of the accident to warn other vehicles, and set up your warning triangle about 50 yards away. If your car catches fire anywhere near your petrol tank, the risk of explosion is considerable, and moving everyone well away from the vehicle quite essential. If the fire is a modest one, and you are quite certain that there is no risk of an explosion, tackling it with a fire extinguisher may be possible if you act quickly.

In Belgium, the police seem to expect to be called to all but the most trivial of accidents, even if no one is injured, and they can insist on everyone remaining at the scene of the accident until they have completed their enquiries, which have been known to take hours. In most other Western European countries, the police

---

### Information needed after an accident

1.   Date, time and place of the accident (ask a local to show you on the map if you were travelling fast and are not exactly sure where you were);
2.   The make, registration number and country of registration of all other vehicles involved;
3.   The name, address, occupation and nationality of each driver involved and some proof of his identity (the number of his passport and/or driving licence);
4.   The name and address of the owner of any vehicles damaged, if the owner was not driving;
5.   The name and address of the insurance companies of any vehicles involved in the accident, the number of the driver's insurance certificate or, if he is driving abroad (such as a Frenchman in Spain), the number of his Green Card;
6.   The name and addresses of any independent witnesses (the legal definition of 'independent' in this context is usually any witness not travelling in any of the vehicles involved and not having a close relationship with any of the parties involved in the accident);
7.   The names and addresses of any passengers or other parties injured and an indication of the probable nature of their injuries;
8.   Details of any damage inflicted on all the vehicles involved, including your own;
9.   If the circumstances of the accident are affected by some mechanical failure or defect, check the condition of brakes, tyres, steering and lights (if appropriate) of all the vehicles involved, as far as you feel competent to do so;
10.   Make a note, for your own personal use later, of the estimated speed of all the vehicles involved, the condition of the road and the weather, and the circumstances of accident (e.g. signals, lack of; speed, excess of, etc);
11.   The name, number and force of any policemen called to the scene of the accident.

---

need be called only if someone has been injured. In Yugoslavia, it is a serious offence not to report an accident (or for that matter, a breakdown) if the vehicle presents any kind of obstruction. As soon as it is practical to do so, you should inform the insurance agent of your insurers in the country in which you are travelling – they will all be listed on the reverse side of your Green Card – and advise your own insurers by telegram or telex.

Although the soundest advice is always never admit anything and never sign anything, if the police are called, particularly in France, this is realistically no longer tenable. The police will produce an accident report form known as a *constat,* which must be completed by all those involved, dated and signed.

### Speeding
Brushes with the police are rather more common as the result of speeding offences. Unlike those in the United Kingdom, the traffic police in much of Western Europe are authorised to fine motorists on the spot. The only exceptions are Greece and Sweden, where fines are payable at special offices; and Finland and Belgium, where fines are paid by going to a post office and purchasing some special stamps. Leaving any of these countries without paying would make a motorist liable to arrest should he return another year. Fines are extremely high – into three figures sterling in many instances – and motorists who can't, or won't pay, must expect their vehicles to be impounded. In Spain there is a 20% discount for immediate settlement, although in practice foreign motorists have very little choice. Any refusal to pay is certain to involve protracted legal proceedings and will probably be to no avail. However a foreign motorist can complete a formal appeal written in his own language within ten days, and this will be considered by the Spanish authorities without any need for him to attend court. The chances of success are slim. Whenever a motorist is fined on the spot, he should insist on an official receipt, and check it carefully to see that the amount he has paid coincides with the figures, as in some countries, in this important respect, a traffic policeman's concentration has been known to wander.

### Breathalyzers
The breath test, *l'alcooltest,* is sometimes administered at random in France, though most frequently after an accident or another offence has already been committed. A huge fine may be administered on the spot, or, if a motorist is substantially over the limit, he may suffer arrest and imprisonment. As a deterrent in the peak summer months, French magistrates sometimes literally hold court in a lay-by, and motorists guilty of serious offences are charged, tried and more often than not convicted on the spot. They could well be suspended from driving immediately and their vehicles impounded until they can be collected by a third party. The inconvenience of this will be apparent to all British motorists, especially as their insurers would be within their rights to refuse to meet the costs of someone crossing the Channel subsequently to collect the car.

### Cash or cheque
As Continental policemen accept cash, cash and only cash in payment of fines, a prudent (or pessimistic) motorist will take a sizeable amount of the appropriate foreign currency to avoid the consequences of speeding becoming even more disagreeable. Another reason for taking a substantial amount of cash is the bewildering banking hours on the Continent. What with fête days and public holidays and bank holidays, which often happen one after the other, Saturday opening and Monday closing, or Monday opening and Saturday closing, relying on a bank is liable to reduce any visitor to bread and water within a week. The only alternative is often the main railway station, where the longer the holiday, the longer the queues.

Travellers' cheques might be seen as a solution to the problem, were it not for the fact that hotels and other establishments convert them at a most unfavourable rate of exchange. In contrast, banks often offer a better rate of exchange than they do for cash, because they like to encourage holidaymakers to take out travellers' cheques. The bank debits their account immediately and has the use of the money until the cheques arrive back from another bank abroad. As many holidaymakers order their travellers' cheques early and sometimes keep some of them until their next trip abroad, the clearing banks enjoy a multi-million interest-free loan from their customers every summer.

The prudent traveller will probably take a mixture of cash and travellers' cheques, relying on his cheque book for emergencies. However it is no longer possible to cash a UK domestic cheque backed only by a UK domestic cheque guarantee card. All the major clearing banks now require their customers who want to cash a cheque in foreign parts to apply for a special Eurocheque encashment card and, in the case of the Midland, Bank of Ireland, Allied Irish, Clydesdale and Northern banks, to take special Eurocheques for use with it as well.

### Medical treatment

A holiday insurance policy is essential not only to cover such contingencies as loss of tickets or money, but also the cost of medical treatment. As holiday insurance premiums cost the same whether or not you want medical cover, there is no reason at all for you to rely on the reciprocal arrangements with other EEC countries.

If, through some mental aberration, you have managed to read leaflet SA 30 published by the Department of Health and Social Security, and have completed the form CM1 inside it to obtain Form E111 before your departure, yet at the same time omitted to take out a standard holiday insurance, this is the process by which you recover some of your medical costs. First, when you visit the doctor, ask him for a slip known as *une feuille de maladie,* and refuse to be fobbed off by suggestions that you obtain one from the local health department office, as this takes ages, and all doctors have a supply tucked away somewhere. Second, pay the doctor's

bill in full – he won't give you a prescription until you do. Third, take the prescription and the *feuille* to the pharmacists, pay for the medicine in full, and see that the price tag on the bottle or tablets, called a *vignette,* is detached from each item and stuck on the *feuille.* Repeat the process for each subsequent visit to doctor and pharmacist. Fourth, find the *bureau de la sécuritée sociale,* the local social security office, and hand over a copy of the doctor's bill and the *feuille de maladie,* complete with the prescription charges stuck on it. Fifth, show them your form E111, but don't forget to ask for it to be returned, in case you need further medical treatment. Sixth, sit back and wait for an international money order for 70% of the bill to arrive by post at your home address in the UK.

### Sensible precautions

As far as your health abroad is concerned, of course, prevention is much better than cure. Typhoid vaccinations are still recommended if you are visiting Spain, Portugal, Yugoslavia or Greece and almost all the Mediterranean islands. To avoid stomach upsets, be particularly careful when offered the following foods: uncooked shellfish, or lightly cooked fish or meat; raw vegetables, salads and unpeeled fruit; cold food and especially reheated food; ice cream, cream, milk (unless you pour it yourself from a pasteurised and sealed bottle), unsealed bottled drinks; yoghurt, and ice cubes. Although tap water is essentially safe in most large cities throughout Europe, the cautious traveller sticks to mineral water, and even cleans his teeth in it. If you stay at a hotel with a refrigerator in the room, empty the ice tray, and replenish it with mineral water. Otherwise avoid iced drinks and keep to those which have simply been chilled, intact, in a refrigerated section of the bar.

The other malady calculated to affect your ability to travel is serious sunburn. While the prevention is obvious, many holidaymakers do seriously underestimate the effect of the sun's rays, especially in apparently cloudy conditions and near to the sea. Wet skin is more easily penetrated by the crucial ultraviolet rays, and water, white buildings, snow, or fine sand, all reflect the sun's rays. Lotions containing calamine relieve the most painful effects, but a tepid bath, followed by aspirin, can help to reduce your temperature and relieve headache.

Another kind of headache follows an excess of alcohol, and is best prevented at the time by drinking a lot of water simultaneously.

**Bites**
Insect bites are irritating and in the case of mosquitoes can in some areas transmit malaria. Biting insects are most prevalent after dark and are attracted by light, perfumes and sweat. If you are bitten, anti-histamine cream will help to reduce the swelling, and bathing in cold water will also relieve the itching. The best prevention is an insect repellant containing diethyl toluamide, sprayed in the room, and on yourself, in considerable quantity. There is, however, a risk that it will also repel humans.

The bites that must cause most concern are from animals. Rabies is a serious danger in eastern France, and no area of the Continent is entirely safe. It is trans-mitted in the saliva of infected animals, so a bite, or even a lick on an existing sore, can result in infection. Identifying the animal and having it watched subsequently

*Insect bites can spoil a holiday*

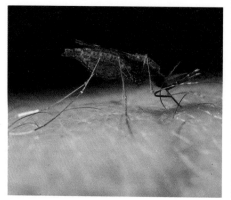

is the only means of calculating the risk. You may need a tetanus injection and at worst the complete course of treatment to prevent rabies, which is in itself extremely painful and unpleasant. Consulting a doctor is vital at the earliest opportunity. This may seem unnecessarily alarmist but, while the chances of catching rabies in Western Europe remain remote, the disease is so appalling that every possible precaution should be taken. Children, especially, should be kept well away from animals, however friendly and domesti-cated they seem.

**Help from the Consul**
If you should ever be arrested, insist on the British Consulate being informed, but do not expect an immediate, miraculous release. When the consul or one of his officers arrives, he will do his best to discover exactly what charges may be laid against you, but he cannot pay for a lawyer to represent you or put up money so that you can be released on bail. All he will do is to contact relatives or friends to explain the difficulty in which you find yourself, and provide a list of lawyers who you, or your relations, could pay to represent you in court.

There is actually a long list of things that a consul cannot do for people in trouble. He cannot pay your hotel, medical or other bills; he cannot give legal advice; he cannot help to trace missing persons; and he cannot use his influence to get you prefer-ential treatment in hospital, prison, or in front of magistrates or judges.

What a consul can do is to issue you with an emergency single-page passport should your own be lost or stolen; contact relations and ask them to send you money; advise on how to transfer funds from the UK; and, in an emergency, advance money against sterling cheques of up to £50 a cheque, provided that it is supported by a banker's card. But it is only as a last resort that the consul will make a loan for repatri-ation to the UK, and then only by taking your passport away (assuming you still have it) and giving you a temporary docu-ment for a single trip, to make almost certain that you will repay the loan in order to recover your passport. He is under no legal obligation in any case to advance money or travel tickets, and he will only do so if he is convinced that you are absolutely destitute and no one can help. In short, the British Consul is unlikely to have heard of the proverb, that he who gives willingly, gives twice.

The busiest British consulates are probably those at the Channel ports, where British citizens with tales of woe from the Pyrenees to Port Said are passed through their hands on the last lap towards repatriation. Here, too, are the hitch-hikers who discover that, however persuasive they are, it is almost impossible to hitch-hike across the Channel: for some inexplicable reason, the ferry companies expect them to buy a ticket. And into the consulate come those embarrassed British motorists who have blown the last franc at the hypermarket, only to miss their ferry.

**Ferry interchange**

Although ferry and hovercraft tickets are not interchangeable, except, that is, on those very rare occasions when the hovercraft service is prevented from operating in bad weather, some flexibility of travel does still exist. Ferry companies will naturally hope that if they cannot squeeze you on one of their ships, either because you omitted to book, or, on extremely rare occasions, you were overbooked and the ship was full, then they will take you on their next sailing. However, unless you have bought a return excursion with a time limit on the trip, it is possible to obtain a refund on unused tickets, though not on the spot. If the interval between sailings with the company you booked with seems too long to wait, simply buy another ticket with another company and apply for a refund on your unused ticket later.

There is, however, something of a dilemma if you are offered the chance to join the standby queue for the original ferry: if you agree to do so, you may in fact get on; but if not, and you want to switch to another company, you would have to go back through passport control

and customs, explaining the rather unusual circumstances, in order to buy a new ticket and begin the process all over again. One rather drastic solution would be, if a place on the first ship cannot be guaranteed when you arrive, to buy a ticket for the second ship before joining the standby queue for the first ship. Then, if you fail to find room on the first, with a little ingenuity it should be possible to transfer to the queue for the second ship, using the other ticket. Of course, if that is also just a standby ticket, you could become that phenomenon – the tripper who never gets beyond the Eastern Docks. . .

**Emergency numbers**
*British consulates*

| | |
|---|---|
| Paris | (1) 26 69 142 |
| Boulogne | (21) 30 25 11 |
| Calais | (21) 96 46 94 |
| | 96 33 76 |
| Dunkerque | (28) 66 11 98 |
| Belgian ports | ring Antwerp: |
| | (03) 32 69 40 |

Outside normal office hours, an answering service will advise callers of the number of the duty officer to contact in a real emergency.

*Banks*
Banks do not provide any emergency service. Contact your own branch direct in business hours; Continental branches of UK banks are unable to offer assistance.

*Credit cards*
Access:

| | |
|---|---|
| 24 hours (except | 0702–338366 |
| Christmas Day) | 0702–352255 |
| American Express: | |
| Mon–Fri 9am–5pm | 0273–696933 |
| 24 hours | 01–222 9633 |
| | 01–551 1111 |
| Diners Club: | 0252–516261 |

Recorded messages outside office hours

| | |
|---|---|
| Visa (Barclaycard): | |
| 24 hours (except | 0604–21100 |
| Christmas Day) | 0604–21288 |
| 7.30am–midnight | 0604–252139 |

# Bringing it back

## Bargains to buy and an explanation of duty-free and customs regulations

*French markets are fun and there may be bargains too*

## Bargain-hunting

It is indeed an ill wind that really does blow nobody any good, and British visitors to France have benefited from the drop in trade that resulted from the ending of identity-card travel. In Calais and Boulogne they have been inundated with gifts, discounts and trading stamps. In Calais, 60 shops have formed themselves into a Shopping Circle, where British customers receive trading stamps worth about £1 for every £30 they spend. Boulogne, whose own Shopping Club with 50 members was formed back in 1981, went one better, with vouchers available on the ferries that reduced prices on many items in the shops by 20 per cent. Supermarkets and department stores make spectacular offers on certain products from time to time, for example, an opportunity to buy 150 bottles of wine for the price of 100.

Even without these special offers, Continental shopping can save a considerable amount of money – always providing, of course, that you intended to purchase the products in the UK in the first place. Boulogne keeps a check on the same 18 items each year to see how far this price advantage is retained. Needless to say, their selection of items is particularly favourable to themselves (but then that is the whole point of shopping there in the first place), and it does also depend on the exchange rate between French francs and sterling. The comparison (see box below) was made between prices in a French supermarket and the equivalent in a British supermarket. Continental weights and measures were used, so in some cases the British prices had to be calculated on a proportional basis; French prices were converted to equivalent sterling prices.

**Suggested purchases**
The items on the list give some indication of 'good buys' in the French ports, but it is by no means exhaustive. There are in fact a great many products available in the Continental ports, both in France and in Belgium, that would cost considerably more in the UK.

**Wine:** Not all wine is cheaper on the Continent, and not all wine is worth buying – a popular misconception among British visitors. The really expensive wines in France, Château Margaux, Château Latour, and so on, may cost as much in France as they do in this country. British duties are levied on the alcoholic content of the wine, not on its value, so the duty on say Château Lafite may be the same as on supermarket 'plonk'.

At the bottom end of the scale, very cheap wine, usually offered for sale in plastic litre bottles, while rarely undrinkable, is not usually worth the effort of carrying it across the Channel except perhaps when bought direct from a co-operative. It will certainly provide a most disappointing taste when removed from its French surroundings. Especially as, if you are really unlucky, it can be a wine that does not travel at all.

If you concentrate on middle-range priced products, the prices will be between half to one third of the cost of a similar bottle bought in the UK. These would include good quality Beaujolais and Muscadet, St Emilion, Bordeaux, Sancerre, Chablis, Pouilly Fuissé and sparkling Saumur. They will always be highly palatable.

Hypermarkets and supermarkets frequently have a special wine offer within this range of wines, which is always worth

| Supermarket prices 1985 | | | |
|---|---|---|---|
| Item | Size | UK | France |
| Olive oil | Litre | 2.60 | 2.10 |
| Sunflower oil (French) | Litre | 1.90 | 1.05 |
| Bottled beer (French) | 2½ litres | 2.30 | 1.47 |
| Mineral water (Perrier) | Litre | 0.50 | 0.37 |
| Casserole dish (Le Creuset) | 'E' | 19.50 | 16.01 |
| Coffee beans | Kilo | 4.60 | 3.26 |
| Box of Camembert | 250g | 0.85 | 0.68 |
| House paté | Kilo | 3.25 | 2.94 |
| Wine vinegar | 75cl | 0.80 | 0.63 |
| French mustard | 300g | 0.49 | 0.25 |
| Sea salt | 500g | 0.35 | 0.26 |
| Tin of 'petit pois' peas | 270g | 0.40 | 0.32 |
| 4 Duralex glasses | 15cl | 1.65 | 0.58 |
| Champagne (Moet & Chandon) | 75cl | 9.40 | 7.14 |
| Côtes du Rhone | 75cl | 2.60 | 0.89 |
| Entre deux Mers | 75cl | 2.40 | 0.95 |
| Pastis | Litre | 9.40 | 7.35 |
| Cointreau | Litre | 9.80 | 6.83 |
| TOTAL | | £72.79 | £53.08 |

considering. As most of their customers are French, despite the number of British visitors, there is no question of it being anything other than genuine, or of the wine being below standard.

Price is one clue to a wine's quality. Another can be the category in which it is placed, indicated on the label. The better wines are marked AC or AOC, or in full, *appellation d'origine controlée*. The type of grape used, the method of production, the amount bottled and the area from which it comes are all closely defined. However, do not suppose that this means that every wine marked in this way is of equal quality. It simply means that their agreed position in the wine hierarchy is controlled by checks on their production.

In fact wines in the second category, marked VDQS, *vins délimités de qualité supérieure,* subject to less stringent checks, can sometimes be better than those at the bottom end of the first.

This may be because the producers are working their way up hoping to reach an AOC classification and are producing a good wine in the lower category. Or it may be that in a good year there is more of an AOC wine than can legally be sold under that classification, so it is being sold as a VDQS wine from that region.

In the third category come *vin de pays,* made from approved varieties of grape in a particular region, usually indicated by the name on the bottle. They are of superior quality to the fourth category, *vin de table,* which is blended wine from several regions, priced according to the alcoholic content, and sold under brand names e.g. Vin Nicolas.

**Beer:** Although prices have risen significantly, beer remains an outstandingly worthwhile purchase in France or Belgium, provided that you do not have to carry it. Although the days are gone when the only restriction on what you could buy was the sum total of, curiously, your allowance for goods other than alcohol, perfume and cigarettes, it would take a determined beer-drinker to get the 50 litres permitted back to his car. French beer is now marketed on an international basis, so names such as Kronenbourg and Kanterbräu are quite familiar in the UK.

**Liqueurs:** those made in France are conspicuously cheaper than in the UK, and often sold in larger, litre bottles, so it is easy to mistake the price. Among the best known are Benedictine (herb–based), Cassis (blackcurrants), Cointreau (oranges), Kirsch (cherries), Calvados (apples) and Chartreuse, both green and yellow, made to a secret monastic formula.

**Fruit syrups:** ideal for making multifarious milk shakes, and extremely popular with children. Grenadine, bright red and derived from pomegranates, is a popular one.

**Mineral water:** in small bottles, for example Perrier, fashionable and pricy, though less so than in the UK. In large bottles you need a lot of room in your car even to consider taking them.

**Coffee:** coffee beans, which can be frozen back in Britain, are around 70% of the UK price.

**Cognac:** one of the great products of France. The best comes from close to the town of that name, two districts called Grande and Petite Champagne. From which it can be deduced that Champagne Cognac is not brandy mixed with champagne. . .

**Cheese:** if you buy camembert, make sure that it is not fully ripe; but there is a prodigious choice of cheeses available.

**Garlic:** obtainable usually in markets in strings or plaits. Much cheaper, but the quality is sometimes indifferent. If the supermarket does stock it, a safer bet.

**Vinegar:** The French love vinegar flavoured by various drinks and fruits. Wine vinegar and cider vinegar are, however, the most palatable for the unitiated.

**Oil:** olive oil comes in several qualities, *vierge* is the best, but it is no longer the great bargain it once was.

**Soups:** delicious fish soup stock in sealed glass containers, or ready-to-eat soups in plastic ones (best eaten soon after your return home); a huge variety of packet soups.

**Mustard:** even more varieties of these.

Dijon is still thought to be the best, especially Maille and Grey Poupon; for presents, try Moutarde de Meaux, which comes in neat little earthenware pots.

**Tinned specialities:** *pâté de foie gras,* goose or duck liver pâté; *cassoulet,* a stew of bean, pork, sausage and garlic; *confit d'oie,* preserved goose; *escargot,* snails; *nougat; petit pois,* little peas.

**Children:** not for sale, however tempting an idea it might seem to some British parents . . . but they are catered for magnificently on the Continent. Clothes and juvenile shoes are not cheaper, but superbly designed; track shoes and plimsolls *are* much cheaper; bars of chocolate are good value and biscuits, if dearer, quite delicious. Toys, especially some for smaller children, such as Lego and Duplex, are an excellent buy; so are children's bicycles, in particular those that convert from four wheels to two once the rider has the knack; for that matter, all bicycles from folding to racing bikes are better value.

**Gardens:** flower seeds and plants (but see p.156) provide rich variety; garden implements, from lawn mowers to watering cans, well designed and good value; decorative pots, urns, statues and balustrades are attractive but could strain your car. Garden furniture, everything from swinging hammocks to trestle tables, are outstanding in design and price. Barbecues in kit form are much cheaper than in the UK.

**DIY:** although the gap between prices is narrowing, tools, especially power tools, are better value than in the UK; but beware of trying to match metric sizes to non-metric tasks back home.

**Kitchens:** Le Creuset casserole dishes are sometimes 30% below the UK price, but be warned: they are extremely heavy to carry. Kitchen knives are of superior quality to many made in Britain, especially the Sabatier brand, which is outstanding. Big breakfast cups, white china, pottery dishes and heavy glasses are also attractive to British shoppers. In the cheaper department stores, a whole range of inexpensive glassware is available, ideal for parties or for use by clumsy children. Excellent kitchen gadgets.

**Dining rooms:** Baccarat crystal glasses, porcelain from Limoges, plates from Gien, china by Villeroy Bosch, cutlery from Thiers. Still expensive though.

**Household linen:** pillows, sheets, eiderdowns, towels, dressing gowns, tablecloths, napkins, tea towels, all beautifully designed and excellent value.

**Stationery:** less expensive, but envelopes are virtually transparent; maps and guides of parts of France cost less; so do pens, crayons, exercise books and satchels.

**Ski equipment:** except at fashionable resorts, ski equipment of all kinds made in France costs less for the same quality.

**Tyres:** In hypermarkets, the tyre prices are lower than even the most relentless cut-price shop in the UK, but do make sure that they fit your make of car, because they won't take them back.

And one commodity that never travels successfully – French bread, however splendid it looks. Unless you actually live in Dover, and take the hovercraft, the bread is always past its best by the time you arrive home. It is not for nothing that the French buy fresh bread at least twice a day: it is simply not baked to last.

# Duty-free

Carrying passengers across the Channel is big business. Sealink, with a capacity of more than 40,000 passengers, are the biggest consortium in the world dealing in the aquatic transportion of people, rather than freight. Townsend Thoresen, with a capacity of more than 20,000, lie fourth.

All the companies sell a huge amount of duty-free goods. Indeed Sealink lie third in the world list of airports, airlines and shipping companies, behind only London's Heathrow and Schipol Airport in Amsterdam. Townsend Thoresen, with a turnover boosted by the acquisition of P & O Ferries, are a close rival – out of a list of literally thousands.

As duty-free goods are a major source of revenue, all the companies were no doubt relieved by the success of their campaign to prevent the EEC from abolishing duty-free concessions altogether. But just how much of a bargain are they for the traveller?

First it must be said that while duty-free prices on ships plying between Dover and the Continent are not the dearest in the world, nor are they the cheapest. The annual review of duty and tax-free prices, "The Best 'n' Most in Drinks, Fragrances and Smokes" uses Schipol Airport, Amsterdam as its starting point, because this is generally the cheapest. The shipping companies are indexed as follows:–

| | |
|---|---|
| Hoverspeed | 130 |
| Sealink | 125 |
| Townsend Thoresen | 123 |
| Sealink (Belgium) | 101 |
| Schipol | 100 |

[For comparison: Heathrow 130]

These data may not be statistically reliable, and some could well be suspect, especially as the Belgian division of Sealink appears separately, but not the Dutch or French divisions. It may come as a surprise to some passengers to discover that while Sealink, even following the sale of Sealink UK to Sealink British Ferries, have maintained uniform fares, such uniformity does not extend to duty-free shops on board. An earlier survey by *Holiday Which* expressed the percentage savings in comparison with the cost of the same goods in the cheapest British shops (see below).

Again, these data may not be statistically reliable, especially as prices in duty-free shops change quite quickly. But it is unlikely that travellers will alter their plans simply because of some small difference in duty-free prices between the companies.

The figures do indicate the considerable

---

### Most popular brands of spirits

1. Chivas Regal '12 years' Whisky
2. Johnnie Walker 'Black Label' Whisky
3. Glenfiddich 'Malt' Whisky
4. Johnnie Walker 'Red Label' Whisky
5. Remy Martin 'V.S.O.P.' Cognac
6. Beefeater Gin
7. Gordon's 'London Dry' Gin
8. Drambuie Liqueur
9. Cointreau Liqueur
10. Bell's 'Extra Special' Whisky

---

difference in the price between individual products, which in turn depends on the volume sold and the price charged by the original manufacturer. In this respect it is often the most popular brands that have a price advantage, and it can pay to be aware of what is purchased most prolifically. (See boxes above).

Not every ship stocks all these products of course, or has them on sale at a low price. For example, although Campari boasts the best distribution among individual wines throughout the world, Sealink had the dubious distinction of selling it at the highest price, more than three times the lowest, at Milan's Linate Airport. Against this, the price advantage on Belgian Sealink ships was helped considerably by some really low prices on perfume, an index rating of 81, considerably cheaper than Amsterdam's Schipol. But when it came to cigarettes, Townsend Thoresen were actually the cheapest. Again, it can pay to buy from among the most popular brands (see box above).

---

### Company by company prices

| | Whisky | Gin | Vodka | Bacardi | Cointreau |
|---|---|---|---|---|---|
| Hoverspeed | 45% | 40% | 30% | 45% | — |
| Sealink (UK) | 45/55% | 40/50% | 30/35% | 45% | 35% |
| Sealink (French) | 45% | 40% | 40% | 70% | 65% |
| Townsend Thoresen | 45/55% | 50% | 30/45% | 40% | 40% |
| Sealink (Belgian) | 55/60% | 55% | 50% | 60% | 65% |

[e.g. 40% = 40 per cent less than UK shop price]

| Most popular brands of cigarettes |
| --- |
| 1. Marlborough Filter |
| 2. Dunhill 'International' Filter |
| 3. Benson & Hedges 'Special' King Size Filter |
| 4. Rothmans King Size Filter |
| 5. John Player 'Special International' Filter |
| 6. Camel Filter |
| 7. Kent King Size Filter |
| 8. Winston Filter |
| 9. Camel Regular |
| 10. Silk Cut King Size |

| Most popular brands of perfumes |
| --- |
| 1. Nina Ricci |
| 2. Chanel |
| 3. Yves Saint Laurent |
| 4. Christian Dior |
| 5. Paco Rabanne |
| 6. Rochas |
| 7. Guy Laroche |
| 8. Givenchy |
| 9. Hermes |
| 10. Carven |
| 11. Jean Patou |
| 12. Estee Lauder |

In perfumes, harassed husbands uncertain of what to buy might be helped by the fact that 'L'Air du Temps', marketed by Parfums Nina Ricci, is the international best seller. Next come Chanel No 5 and an Yves Saint Laurent product, 'Opium'. However, as the lines sold generally change every year, and there are nearly 9,000 different products on the market, it is the list of leading brand names that may prove the most useful (see box above).

On most ferries out of Dover, a booklet will be available listing the brands of perfumes, wine, spirits and cigarettes available in the duty-free shops on board – though not their prices, as these, alas, would soon be out of date. But the booklet is extremely useful for making your own price list, in sterling, or, better still, in the currency of the country where you are going. Remember also to make a note of the size of the bottles, because litre and half litre bottles are common on board ship, less common in shops on land. Also, when comparing prices, remember that standard bottles back in the UK usually vary between 70 and 75cl, and that duty-free vermouth is often found in bottles of 95cl, not a full litre.

But from now on, you need a calculator – buy one on the ship if you have forgotten to bring one, as they will be free of V.A.T. Without a calculator, you will find it extremely tiresome to answer the key questions on what and where to buy:
– at your destination in the holiday areas;
– at the Channel ports before boarding the ferry or hovercraft home;
– duty-free on the way back.
If you are driving to Scandinavia, the first choice can be eliminated immediately. Wines and spirits are incredibly expensive, in some cases twice as much as the UK price. Elsewhere, however, the local prices may surprise you (see box below).

Needless to say, you may have to hunt around to find prices as low as these. If you buy tax-paid goods in an EEC country you are entitled to bring back half as much again as your duty-free allowance (see

### Country by country prices

| Country | Whisky | Gin | Vodka | Bacardi | Cointreau | Drambuie | Cigarettes |
| --- | --- | --- | --- | --- | --- | --- | --- |
| Belgium | 20% | 30% | 15% | 25% | 40% | 35% | 35% |
| France | 25% | 30% | 20% | 45% | 45% | 35% | 40% |
| Italy | 55% | 45% | 60% | 55% | 65% | 60% | 45% |
| Spain | 30% | 35% | 75% | 70% | 65% | 30% | 30% |
| West Germany | 30% | 35% | 35% | 40% | 60% | 35% | 20% |

[40% = 40 per cent cheaper than UK shop price]

p.155). So if you can buy at or around the ship-board prices you will do better by buying on the Continent rather than on board ship. You are likely to find that the following is generally true:

Cigarettes: slightly cheaper than duty-free prices in Italy; about the same in Belgium and France.
Whisky: cheaper in Italy than duty-free
Gin: cheaper in Italy than duty-free; about the same in Spain
Vodka: cheaper in Spain and Italy; about the same in West Germany
Bacardi: cheaper in Spain; slightly cheaper in Italy and France

Cointreau: generally cheaper than duty-free
Drambuie: cheaper in Italy than duty-free; about the same in France.

Much of course depends on whether you are travelling by car, because some of the savings do not amount to all that much in real terms and have to be weighed up – almost literally – against the inconvenience of carrying bottles which somehow seem to become heavier and heavier as the day progresses. There is also the not inappreciable risk of dropping the lot, which could wipe out your gains in a moment, however clever you have been with a calculator.

# Customs

When you drive off the ship or hovercraft at Dover, you will be directed first to Immigration, where your passports will be examined, in all probability without any need for you to get out of the car; and then to the Customs Hall; the last obstacle before the homeward journey.

Many holidaymakers are at best confused by the duty-free allowances on their return to the UK, and at worst expect the forthcoming examination by a customs officer to be a frightening experience. In reality, if they take the trouble to work out what they are allowed to bring back, and make an honest declaration, they have nothing at all to worry about. Customs officers are not sadistic individuals who delight in leaving the head of a family a quivering wreck or marching him off in handcuffs clutching his one bottle over the limit. They are really on the lookout for professional smugglers of prohibited items such as narcotics, and would much prefer to wave the holidaymaker on his way.

If you elect to go through the 'Green' channel which indicates that you have nothing over the limit to declare, they will usually ask a few perfunctory questions before allowing you through. If you drive into the 'Red' channel, the customs officer will be expecting a clear description of what dutiable goods you are bringing back.

The members of the EEC are Belgium, Denmark, France, West Germany, Greece, Irish Republic, Italy, Luxembourg, the Netherlands, and the United Kingdom. Spain and Portugal should join shortly. Austria, Switzerland, Norway, Sweden and the Channel Islands, for example, are not part of the EEC community.

The Customs and Excise definition of spirits includes brandy, gin, rum, whisky and vodka. Most liqueurs are usually over the 38.8% proof limit and count therefore as spirits, but *cassis, fraise,* advocaat and most apéritifs are nearly always below. Fortified wines include madeira, port, sherry and vermouth.

Although you have the option of buying, in the EEC, up to three litres of sparkling wine, you can substitute three litres of still wine to make a total of seven litres, if you buy no other alcohol. As most French wine is sold in 75cl bottles, a customs officer is unlikely to make much fuss if you take ten bottles in all, strictly speaking, half a bottle more than your actual allowance.

While you can buy, say, your perfume in a French shop, and your cigarettes duty-free, you are not allowed to mix categories within the same broad section. For

# Your allowances

| Goods bought in a duty or tax-free shop in the EEC or on a ferry or hovercraft OR goods obtained outside the EEC | | Goods bought where the purchase price includes EEC duty and taxes |
|---|---|---|
| **TOBACCO** | | |
| 200 | Cigarettes | 300 |
| | OR | |
| 100 | Cigarillos | 150 |
| | OR | |
| 50 | Cigars | 75 |
| | OR | |
| 250 gm | Tobacco | 400 gm |
| **ALCOHOL** | | |
| 1 litre | Spirits over 38.8% proof | 1.5 litres |
| | OR | |
| 2 litres | Spirits under 38.8% proof | 3 litres |
| | OR | |
| 2 litres | Fortified or sparkling wine | 3 litres |
| | AND | |
| 2 litres | Still table wine | 4 litres |
| **PERFUME** | | |
| 60cc or 2 fl oz | | 90cc or 3 fl. oz |
| **TOILET WATER** | | |
| 240cc or 9 fl. oz. | | 375cc or 13 fl. oz |
| **OTHER GOODS** | | |
| £28 value | | £163 value |

example, if you buy a litre of spirits on a ferry, you will be permitted only the duty-free limit on still wine, irrespective of whether you purchased it on the boat or in an EEC shop.

If you plan to bring back still or sparkling wine in excess of your duty-free allowance, you must declare it and pay both excise duty and V.A.T. The duty will be the following:

| Bottle size | Still wine | Sparkling wine |
|---|---|---|
| 70cl | 72p | £1.20 |
| 75cl | 78p | £1.28 |
| 1 litre | £1.04 | £1.71 |

Plus V.A.T. at 15% on the shop price.

Wine is a conspicuously good buy, but outside your allowance, the duty and V.A.T. on other alcohol is likely to bring it close to, or even in excess of, prices charged in UK off-licences. There is, however, one exception: beer, which is not placed in the alcohol category for the purpose of allowances or excise duty. But you are allowed to bring in only 50 litres without duty, a restriction introduced when groups of young men spotted the loophole in the system and took a van across the Channel to stock up on enough booze to last them from one Christmas to the next.

Although there is a limit on perfume and toilet water, in practice this is so high, that you would have to plan to spend a small fortune to be in danger of exceeding it.

One other category in the traditional allowances list has a specific restriction: you are allowed to bring back only 25 lighters, another item that costs much less on the other side of the Channel.

If you were to buy 'other goods' in a duty-free shop or even outside the EEC on a long trip, the limit is still £28 a person. Within the EEC, the limit on other goods was raised at the beginning of July, 1984 from £120 to £163, a further encouragement for purchases to be made tax-paid in EEC countries rather than in duty-free shops, where the allowance remained unchanged.

Visitors to EEC countries can claim exemption from Value Added Tax (known in France and Belgium as T.V.A.) on single items costing roughly the equivalent of £100 or more. Many of the larger and more up-market shops offer this service, although you cannot insist that they do so. What happens is that rather like buying wine at the Porte de Bercy in Paris, you pay the tax in full but are given a copy of the sales receipt to enable you to claim it back. This must be handed over to a customs official as you leave the Continent, and in all probability he will also want to see the items on which you are claiming, to satisfy himself that they are, in fact, being taken abroad. Apart from this potentially time-consuming requirement, there is another catch. These goods for which you have claimed T.V.A. exemption now come into the tax-free category with its £28 limit, above which, of course, excise duty and tax are restored. The conclusion would seem to be that only a purchase of use collectively to a family will avoid duty and tax in the long run.

The import of livestock is strictly forbidden under anti-rabies legislation, whose penalties can include destruction of the animals and imprisonment for humans. But up to five plants may be brought back to Britain, provided that they are not chrysanthemums, fruit trees or bulbs. Although the Colorado beetle rules out potatoes, you are allowed to bring into the UK 2 kilograms of other fruit and vegetables, 1 kilogram of cooked meat, and 1 kilogram of fresh meat – except pork or poultry or offal. It seems safe to predict, however, that few holidays will end by taking offal over to Dover.

## Package Tours

**Belgium**

| Company | Telephone number | Destinations |
|---|---|---|
| Belgian Travel Service | 0902–661171 | Ghent, Bruges, Ostende |
| Belgium Villa Centre | 01–651 5109 | De Panne |
| Car Holidays Abroad | 0992–59939 | Bruges |
| City Fair Holidays | 0234–217766 | Bruges, by rail and Jetfoil |
| Club Continental | 0708–752222 | Ostende Carnival, Bruges |
| Golden Rail Holidays | 0904–28992 | Ostende, Bruges by rail and Jetfoil |
| Hoverspeed | 01–554 7061 | Bruges |
| Sandpiper Holidays | 051–931 2826 | De Haan (s/c) |
| Sealink Holidays | 01–388 6798 | Bruges, Ostende, Ghent |
| Stephen Walker Holidays | 0205–52555 | Ostende, Bruges by rail |
| Time Off | 01–235 8070 | Bruges by rail |
| Townsend Thoresen | 0732–365437 | Bruges, Ghent |
| Transeurope | 0702–351451 | Belgian coast, Bruges, Ostende |
| Victor Holidays | 0378–76451 | Belgian coast, Ostende |

**Northern France**

| Company | Telephone number | Destinations |
|---|---|---|
| Billington Travel | 0732–460666 | Le Touquet, Montreuil, St Omer, Boulogne |
| Burstin Travel | 0702–613011 | Boulogne |
| Car Holidays Abroad | 0992–59939 | Le Touquet |
| French Travel Service | 01–828 8131 | Boulogne, Le Touquet |
| Golden Rail Holidays | 0904–28992 | Boulogne |
| Hoverspeed | 01–554 7061 | Boulogne, Le Touquet |
| Sealink Holidays | 01–388 6798 | Boulogne, Calais, St Omer |
| Time Off | 01–235 8070 | Boulogne, Le Touquet |
| Townsend Thoresen | 0732–365437 | St Omer, Amiens |
| Travelounge/David Newman | 0903–754818 | Lille, Le Touquet |
| Vacances Franco-Britanniques | 0242–35515 | Calais, Montreuil |

This list is not intended to be exhaustive, nor are the holidays provided by these or any other companies necessarily good value for money; they are simply representative of what is available. Tours and companies may change at short notice. Places mentioned are not necessarily all that is offered in northern France or in Belgium by the company concerned.

# Index
## (numbers in italics refer to illustrations)

**Illustration credits**